101
WAYS TO
HELP PEOPLE
IN NEED

STEVE AND JANIE SJOGREN

NAVPRESS®

BRINGING TRUTH TO LIFE

OUR GUARANTEE TO YOU

We believe so strongly in the message of our books that we are making this quality guarantee to you. If for any reason you are disappointed with the content of this book, return the title page to us with your name and address and we will refund to you the list price of the book. To help us serve you better, please briefly describe why you were disappointed. Mail your refund request to: NavPress, P.O. Box 35002, Colorado Springs, CO 80935.

The Navigators is an international Christian organization. Our mission is to reach, disciple, and equip people to know Christ and to make Him known through successive generations. We envision multitudes of diverse people in the United States and every other nation who have a passionate love for Christ, live a lifestyle of sharing Christ's love, and multiply spiritual laborers among those without Christ.

NavPress is the publishing ministry of The Navigators. NavPress publications help believers learn biblical truth and apply what they learn to their lives and ministries. Our mission is to stimulate spiritual formation among our readers.

NAVPRESS, BRINGING TRUTH TO LIFE, and the NAVPRESS logo are registered trademarks of NavPress. Absence of ® in connection with marks of NavPress or other parties does not indicate an absence of registration of those marks.

Cover design by Jennifer Mahalik
Cover photos by Adobe Image Library
Creative Team: Brad Lewis, Amy Spencer, Pat Miller

Some of the anecdotal illustrations in this book are true to life and are included with the permission of the persons involved. All other illustrations are composites of real situations, and any resemblance to people living or dead is coincidental.

Unless otherwise identified, all Scripture quotations in this publication are taken from the HOLY BIBLE: NEW INTERNATIONAL VERSION® (NIV®). Copyright © 1973, 1978, 1984 by International Bible Society. Used by permission of Zondervan Publishing House. All rights reserved. Other versions used include *The New Testament in Modern English* (PH), J. B. Phillips Translator, © J. B. Phillips 1958, 1960, 1972, used by permission of Macmillan Publishing Company.

Library of Congress Cataloging-in-Publication Data

Sjogren, Steve, 1955-
  101 ways to help people in need / Steve & Janie Sjogren.
    p. cm.
Includes index.
  ISBN 1-57683-315-1
  1. Church work with the poor. 2. Caring--Religious
aspects--Christianity. 3. Community--Religious aspects--Christianity.
I. Title: One hundred and one ways to help people in need. II. Title:
One hundred one ways to help people in need. III. Sjogren, Janie, 1954-
IV. Title.
  BV639.P6 S545 2002
  261.8'32--dc21

                                    2002002122

Printed in the United States of America

2 3 4 5 6 7 8 9 10 / 09 08 07 06 05

FOR A FREE CATALOG OF NAVPRESS BOOKS & BIBLE STUDIES,
CALL 1-800-366-7788 (USA) OR 1-800-839-4769 (CANADA)

TO JIM AND DANA COCHRAN

*Thanks for having
a huge heart for those in need—
including us!*

Contents

LEVEL 2: RECONCILIATION—SEEING PEOPLE GET RIGHT WITH GOD AND ONE ANOTHER

ACKNOWLEDGMENTS

THANKS TO THE MANY who have influenced our thinking and behavior during the past fifteen-plus years in the area of caring for people in need. Without your loving influence, the idea of caring for the needy would never have entered our hearts. This list includes Bernie and Bobbi Stevens, John and Pam Bertram, Dave and Debbie Cain, Matthew and Lisa Dyer, Bob and Nola Clark, Vicki Baird, Darla Robinson, Dave and Anita Workman, Bruce and Sandy Ullrey, Walt Witham, Kelly and Mary Wiseman, Kirk and Jane Wiseman, Mary Smith, Dennis and Rose Watson, Dennis and Judy Schumacher, John and Carol Wimber, and Todd and Debbie Hunter.

A hearty thanks to the thousands of amazing people who make up the Vineyard Community Church in Cincinnati. You are always up for a wild (and sometimes seemingly crazy) idea when it comes to caring for the needy. Who says Cincinnatians are conservative? It's certainly not apparent from your track record when it comes to reaching out to the community. This book reads like a "been there, done that" history of VCC over the past sixteen years of our history together. What a start for a church; yet, as we have often said, the best is yet to come. We fully believe, when it comes to the needy, *the best history is yet to be written!*

A big thanks to the many ministry leaders across the country who helped in the research involved in putting this book together, including Jude Del Hierro, Tanya Worsham, Sean Davis, Cheryl Bender, Robbi Sluder, Dan Bernard, Steve Andry, Barb Slavinski, Lori Arnold, Linda Kimble, and Sandi Horine.

INTRODUCTION

WELCOME TO AN ADVENTURE in generosity! When you begin to care for people in need, you're in for an amazing, enriching experience! But be warned: It's one whose benefits you might not easily appreciate or quickly understand. In fact, much of ministry to people with needs is like an experience I (Steve) had in elementary school.

When I was just starting the fourth grade, my friend Wayne and I noticed that a girl in our class was named Gertrude Dorcas Smith (not her real last name, but the first and middle names were real). Wayne and I saw it as our unofficial duty to notice and point out the physical or name oddities of each student. "Gertrude" was bad enough, but her middle name absolutely begged for a good teasing from us. And as insensitive nine-year-old boys, we gladly obliged.

Of course, we didn't have any concept of this girl's many redeeming qualities. As the school year progressed, it was apparent that she was easily the most caring, generous person in the fourth grade. She was the best listener. She was sensitive and a genuine servant. We just enjoyed being in the spotlight for a little bit at the expense of a little girl whose character ran far deeper than both of ours put together.

I lost track of Ms. Gertrude Dorcas, but I wouldn't be surprised if she went on to big things in the kingdom of God. Why? She had the spirit, and better, the name for it. Dorcas was a character of the New Testament whom we call a "ship passing in the night." We don't know much about her, but what little we do know causes us to want to be like her when we grow up. She lived a life of practical good works aimed at caring for those in need. When she died rather suddenly, all those she touched by her many good actions felt an unspeakable, great loss.[1] I have sometimes wondered, "Would I be missed if I suddenly died? Do my actions speak beyond my physical presence?"

God has put into the hearts of all Christians the desire to make a difference in this world. Even if it is deeply buried, he has put into you the desire to serve people who are less well off than you. If you're one of those who senses that desire and you want to make a difference in this world—if you're one who is a Gertrude Dorcas in the making—this book is for you!

The average person can be involved in hundreds of ways to care for the needy. Mother Teresa said that it isn't necessary to move to Calcutta to do something significant for those in need, and she was correct. Needy people are all around you.

When we began to plant churches, the first thing we did to learn to get the heart of God for people was to begin caring for the needy.

We didn't understand what we were doing. But we saw from Scripture that this activity was a high priority for Jesus, so we decided it needed to be a high priority for us as well.

How **Not** to Care for the Needy

My first attempt at caring for the needy was marked with more mistakes than successes. Frankly, I (Steve) didn't have the foggiest idea what I was doing. A number of guys who were eager to do outreach to the needy went with me. It was a Christmas Eve and the weather was bitterly cold.

We knocked at the door of a house that looked like it could use some help. We heard someone inside unfasten several deadbolts and a couple of chain guards. The door opened and a woman stood there with a multitude of children around her feet.

I just said the first thing that came to mind: "Are you poor?"

The mom's eyes grew big and she said, "Well, that's a pretty dumb way to say it, but yes, we could use some help." Fortunately, everyone quickly forgot my off-putting comment when we walked in with our "Christmas in a box" outreach. We happened to be the right people at the right place at the right time.

The father of this family was a drunk and had left a week before Christmas on a drinking binge. Their living room had no connection with the holiday season. We brought in a tree, ornaments, a complete Christmas dinner, and a couple of presents for each child (we'd bought generic presents in advance for boys and girls of various age groups).

In spite of our awkward start, it was a touching first effort at reaching out to someone with needs. By the time we prayed upon leaving, everyone had tears in their eyes—the family we were serving and the men in the group. More importantly, we were hooked. We'd tasted a bit of what it's like to do something practical for others in need, and we saw their eyes light up when a few of their immediate needs were met.

Why Should We Care for the Needy?

It's the normal thing for Christians to do.
Many Christians worldwide are needy themselves. According to Larry Eskridge of the Institute for the Study of American Evangelicals at Wheaton College, "For the first time in history, Christianity has become a religion mainly of the poor, the marginalized, the powerless and—in parts of Asia and the Middle East—the oppressed."[2]

When New Testament writers call us to care for one another, they are calling for us to care for the needy.

Jesus considered it normal for believers to reach out to the poor and needy. Even if you know you should care for the poor, you may not know where to start. Or maybe you're afraid of the unknown. Perhaps you don't know how to cross the bridge into the hearts of the needy. This book is written to empower ordinary people like you and me to find ways to reach people in need.

It feels good.
In *Desiring God: Meditations of a Christian Hedonist* (Multnomah, 1996), pastor and author John Piper says God is a God of experiences. There's nothing wrong with experiential Christianity. In fact, that's the way God intended your faith to work. But like many others, maybe you've been too shy to experience good feelings. There may be nothing more fulfilling than caring for the needy.

It's part of the message of the kingdom.
Most of the time, we've been too binary in our view of the church's mission. We're either the proclaiming church *or* the healing church. But we're supposed to be doing both of these. If we aren't a "both-and" church, we're simply loving in word but not in deed. That sort of love is not genuine according to Jesus.

It causes you to see as God sees.
Be honest. You probably get tired from showing mercy and kindness. God doesn't. When you're seeing as God sees, you'll certainly still grow tired physically—even spiritually—after you've given more than you've taken in. But you'll also be energized in the work of seeing the beginning of transformation of human souls into Christlikeness.

It proves to the watching world that you really are a follower of Christ.

Millions of people are watching Christians collectively to see if Christians are for real—and more importantly, to see if God is for real. In his recent book *Re-Churching the Unchurched*, George Barna made the startling declaration based on his research that only 2 percent of those who don't attend church stay away because they don't believe in God. The other 98 percent stay away because they, for a variety of reasons, don't like what they see when they look at the church.[3] Your actions toward people in need can go a long way toward demonstrating to the skeptics what authentic Christianity looks like, whether it's seen up-close or from a distance.

Most of all—you need "them" more than they need you!

When Jesus said, "The poor you will always have with you," he was promising renewal and continual employment for the church.

As we and our friends have given care to people with needs, we've been blessed to see them change. But the unanimous testimony among those of us doing the serving is, "*We* have been changed by these utterly amazing people!"

The feeling is similar to the one expressed in this letter to Ann Landers from a reader who discovers a surprise in a most unexpected place.

Dear Ann Landers:
I read the letter from "Toni in Texas," whose father gave "useless junk" as gifts to his child.

My father gave me a peculiar gift when I turned 16. It was a well-used physics book in a brown paper bag. He said it would be useful since I was now studying physics in school. I began to question his sanity as he extolled the features of the text.

I dutifully looked at the table of contents. My mother had a hard time trying not to break out in laughter as I tried to fake interest. Dad told me to check out the graphs and charts, so I flipped through the battered book. To my surprise, I found a crisp $2 bill on each page. My father stood there with the smug knowledge that he had taught me not to judge a book by its cover—literally.

Maybe "Toni" should look deeper and see if there is wisdom in her father's gifts.

—LEE IN TEXAS

Dear Lee: How true. I wonder how many children might have tossed the book before seeing the gift inside.[4]

WHY IS IT SOMETIMES HARD TO CARE FOR THE NEEDY?
We expect to get them out of poverty—today!
Some of the needy you'll encounter have needs for just a short time. Others have been in that state for a long time and may be there for the rest of their lives. It's all they've ever known, and it's a cold fact that you really can't do anything to "fix" them. That could be difficult because it goes against the grain of our American way of thinking and even a codependent attitude that says, "Anyone can be changed with enough work."

To give care and love to people in order to fix them is a form of conditional love. It isn't the way God loves and it isn't the way he invites people into his family.

We want to completely change the world—today!
Perhaps you'll never absolutely, totally change the world. But you will make a difference.

It is estimated that Mother Teresa personally picked up thirty thousand dying people to bring into her hospice to die with dignity. Some may say, "What difference did it make? They were going to die anyway." To that we say, she most definitely made a difference to each one she carried.

That's the perspective you need to have as you care for the needy. You're never going to bring heaven to earth more, better, or faster by ministering to people with needs. But you are absolutely going to change the world one life at a time as you move forward and encounter the next person God places in front of you. The line that the good Mother was fond of using was, "A small thing done with great love . . ." We've taken to finishing that sentence: *"A small thing done with great love will change the world."* That's what Jesus is calling you to in this life.

> *"We take great care of the dying. I am convinced that even one moment is enough to ransom an entire miserable existence, an existence perhaps believed to be useless. All souls are precious to Jesus, who paid for them with his blood."[5]*
> —MOTHER TERESA

When we began to work with others to reach out to people with needs, a lot of days were disappointing. The discouragement came whenever we focused on the most successful days and realized we weren't living up to those. But then we decided that we could establish our lives on a day when we were feeling the least successful working with needy people. This decision came at a time when our team was spending a lot of money and pouring a lot of creative energy into caring for these special people. But it wasn't very apparent whether we were making any real progress. So we decided to shift our perspective.

The shift came about, in part, through a thought expressed by Richard Nixon. He discovered that when you have a new idea and you have talked and talked it up with people to the point that you are just about sick of talking about it—and no one seems to be getting that new idea—that's when people are just beginning to get the new idea. Nixon was onto a profound truth. This observation seems to play itself out in my experience with new ideas and the change process, especially when it comes to caring for the needy. We realized that the people of our own church needed a shift in their perspective.

We've been called to care for the needy, not necessarily to fix all the problems of the poor or to fix the system that's causing them to be poor. What did Jesus mean when he said, "The poor you will always have with you"? We think he was saying that even with all our best efforts, the reality of poverty can't be erased. He calls us to care for people's needs, not to eradicate the problem of poverty.

We want to bring them into the kingdom—today!
The needy are streetwise. They can read through motives behind your actions more quickly than the average person. If they perceive that you're seeing them as a potential notch in your salvation belt, they may play the game overtly, but their hearts will be offended. Don't use acts of mercy and generosity as a means only to "close the deal" or "pray the prayer" or "save" each person you touch. Focus on demonstrating God's love and your own love for them. They'll respond quickly enough and they'll eventually ask what makes you different. The concept of following Christ will come up sooner rather than later.

WHERE ARE THE NEEDY?
They're all around you, but they're often disguised. They blend easily into the scenery of life, and you can miss their cries and faces. The obvious ones are the drug addicts and the homeless you see asking for money. Less obvious are people who are recently divorced, single parents, the elderly, the unemployed or

underemployed, and runaways.

Just down the street from our facility (Vineyard Community Church) on the north side of Cincinnati, we have an amazing array of people with a diversity of needs. To the side of one entrance we have literally million-dollar estates whose pool cabanas are larger than our house! By another entrance are apartments with mostly Central and South Americans who deal with financial and literacy challenges. Down the street about a block is a retirement condo complex with folks who need to know that someone still cares as issues of aging creep upon them.

It's not hard to find people with needs if you just look around your environment.

"At the end of our lives, we will not be judged by how many diplomas we have received, how much money we have made or how many great things we have done. We will be judged by 'I was hungry and you gave me to eat. I was naked and you clothed me. I was homeless and you took me in.'

"Hungry not only for bread— but hungry for love.

"Naked not only for clothing— but naked of human dignity and respect.

"Homeless not only for want of a room of bricks—but homeless because of rejection.

"This is Christ in distressing disguise."[6]

—Mother Teresa

How Did the Needy Become Needy?
Oppression by the Evil One
Jesus stated that he came "to release the oppressed" (Luke 4:18). Part of that oppression is the grip of poverty.

Bad Choices
We've all made bad choices in life. And for some reason, some have made bad choices that have caused more serious consequences. It's important that we don't judge others for the way life has treated them. As the saying goes, "But for the grace of God, there go I."

Oppression by Unfair Social and Political Systems
My grandma used to call them "sitchiations"—something that we get into but just can't get out of. We have all gotten ourselves into a sitchiation now and then, but some people seem to be in them all the time. Their situation is more than bad luck; it's oppression by the systems that operate around them.

WHO ARE THE NEEDY?

Single Parents

Regardless of financial status, being a single parent is a great challenge. Being a single parent doesn't necessarily mean someone is needy, but the probability of being in need increases dramatically when a spouse is removed from the picture.

The church needs to surround families that have been displaced, but it often doesn't know what to do with such situations.

How Do We Define "Poverty"?

"'Basically we are asking the question, if we look back to last year, how many families were not able to purchase food, clothing, shelter, utilities and a little bit more—that basic bundle,' said Kathleen Short, a senior researcher at the Census Bureau.

"While the Census Bureau struggles to define a poverty formula more realistic than the present one, ad hoc poverty measurements pop up frequently from academic institutions, nonprofit organizations, and regional development groups. Nearly all conclude that at the turn of the century, a family of four needs at least $25,000 a year to afford the basics, including a car to commute to work, an item overlooked in the Census Bureau's measure. At least $25,000 is the income featured in the 'basic needs' budget developed by Indiana's Economic Development Council, one goal being to draw jobs to the state that pay at least that much.

"'That is self-sufficiency,' said David Weinschrott, a United Way director. 'Poverty is all about stereotypes. Families with less than $25,000 fall below self-sufficiency.'"[7]

—LOUIS UCHITELLE, NEW YORK TIMES

Working Needy

This group is a surprising and fairly well-disguised population of the poor. Sometimes, these are intact families. Or they may be single parents trying to make it without the assistance of government programs. Generally, these are people who are trying to make a difference, but the odds are seemingly stacked against them.

Uninsured or Underinsured

Millions of Americans walk the tightrope of living without health insurance. They are living an accident away from financial ruin.

And sometimes people who are underinsured have it worse than the uninsured in the United States. At least the uninsured have some government nets to fall back on in many cases. Underinsured people may have insurance, but the deductible amount is so high that they would have to have a virtual financial and health crisis for their insurance to kick in and for them to begin to receive any benefit from it.

> *"Poverty is really the lack of freedom to have or to do basic things that you value. By that definition, a ghetto family that wants to move to an adequate neighborhood but cannot afford to do so, or is prevented by discrimination from doing so, is impoverished."*[8]
>
> —AMARTYA SEN, NOBEL LAUREATE IN ECONOMICS

Elderly

"Old" is a relative issue, especially with baby boomers coming of age. Boomers are edging ever closer to official retirement age. It doesn't take a prophet to predict that this group will change the face of retirement, just as they've altered the look of every social structure they've encountered so far. While many boomers will retire with significant wealth (and some already have), many analysts are predicting that much of this generation will need to work into their eighties to be able to afford retirement. What a scenario!

> ### How Widespread Is Poverty?
>
> *The richest nation in history has persistent, widespread poverty. In 1999, 32.3 million Americans found themselves below the poverty level and 44 million were without health insurance.*[9]

Disabled

I (Steve) am a person with a disability myself. Before my injury, I never noticed how many people had physical handicaps. It has also made me realize that for most of us, it doesn't take much of a disability to get us to a point of dependence upon others for day-to-day survival.

Homeless

People who are homeless are more present and visible in some places than in others. The homeless flavor differs from city to city. Some homeless people are "seasonal" and follow the weather patterns. For example, you don't see a lot of homeless people in Syracuse in the dead of winter, but as the summer rolls around, they appear. San Francisco has a year-round homeless population. Portland has a younger homeless population that is quite large.

Mentally Unstable

Many types of people experience psychological challenges that cause them to be needy. Some who experience significant mental illness would have been permanently hospitalized a few decades ago, but now, due to government cuts in programs, they are freed to their own recognizance. In my experience, the most common mental illness among needy people, and a very common malady in America, is Bipolar Disorder (manic depression). Kay Redfield Jamison backs up this observation in the very interesting book *An Unquiet Mind* (Random House, 1997). If we are going to care for the needy, we need to be aware of the specific needs of the mentally challenged.

Permanently Hospitalized

The first batch of baby boomers to be sent into permanent-care homes will enter those institutions in 2010—not long from now. These will be the poor in spirit, the depressed, and the forgotten. Aside from issues of insurance coverage, many will be dealing with issues of loss and abandonment.

SOME DOS AND DON'TS IN MINISTRY TO THE NEEDY

Be graceful—don't categorize people with needs.

Many people in need have been in their situation just a short time or may be temporarily in their current state.

Don't call them "needy" or "poor," and don't think of them as being in a permanent state of neediness. To do that will cause you to lose hope for them and will affect the way you relate to them.

Who knows—you may be needy someday. A disability could strike you, and certainly you're growing older and could hit "elderly" status some day.

Be outgoing—smile a lot!

Your smile is your most powerful tool for good. If you ever find yourself in a situation where you don't know what to do, try smiling. It almost always defuses tension.

Be true—check your motives and prejudices before leaving home.

Don't go to gawk.

If you're new to ministry to the needy, go over this entire list of dos and don'ts. We have found that without adequate training, embarrassing things happen. For example, when African Americans from our church go out with our teams, newcomers sometimes think they're part of the urban neighborhood we're serving.

Prejudices can come through easily unless your church provides some sensitivity training.

Be bold—don't hesitate to pray for people.
When should you pray? Before, during, and after an outing!

Pray for the people you're ministering to. Of all the folks in the world, the needy are typically the most responsive to prayer. As Jesus said, "How happy are those who know their need of God" (Matthew 5, PH).

We approach them directly and ask, "Do you have any needs we can pray for? May we pray for you right now?"

Be prudent—don't give money to the needy, at least not your own money.
It's easy for codependency to form when you're ministering to the needy. Many churches that have ongoing ministries to people with needs set up a committee to review needs and requests for funds. You might consider creating an application for assistance that not only will help you assess needs, but also will create a database for following up on the person requesting assistance.

Most often, don't give money directly to someone requesting assistance. Instead, pay to the apartment complex, utility company, or car repair shop.

Be careful—don't make promises.
Even subtle promises could be mistaken as written-in-stone commitments by someone in need.

Stay away from statements like, "We'll do this," "We'll be back," or even, "We'll try to . . ." Unless you are the decision-maker in charge and you are absolutely sure, it's better to say something like, "I can see you have a need. I'll check into that. I'm not making you a promise! I'll see what comes up." It's kinder to be noncommittal or even to answer with a definite "no" than to imply a promise of future help and not follow through.

Be a team player.
Personally, I (Steve) have never felt a moment's danger while being around homeless people, the poor, and others with needs. But clearly, it's prudent to do any of these ministries to the needy in teams of two or more. We know of ministries where negative incidents have occurred—always where an individual was overly trusting and alone in a ministry situation.

Be smart—don't get involved in an extreme ministry of generosity without a substantial team behind you.

Newcomers to ministry to the needy often go through a honeymoon period of six months to a year. During this time, they sometimes make unreasonable commitments to ministry to the needy. God has given them a clear love for the needy, but they're a little intoxicated with their love and they lack reasonable boundaries.

As leaders, we have never supported an individual or small group that has an enormous vision for a new outreach to the needy. We know that sounds antithetical to the intent of this book, but after doing this for nearly twenty years, we're fully aware of the immense amount of energy it takes to begin a significant ministry to the oppressed. It's a lot like a whaling operation. It takes a lot of energy, equipment, and an indomitable spirit to succeed, but amateurs are ill advised to harpoon Moby Dick from a little rowboat. He's bigger than you and he will take you where he wants to go. So it is with beginning a significant new ministry to the needy.

Be creative—try out new ideas.

Dare to brainstorm with others and encourage "out of the box" thinking. The great thing about the needy is that they're resilient and forgiving even if something goes slightly wrong with your approach.

Be hungry—hang around the needy in order to receive the empowering of the Holy Spirit.

We spend time with the needy to get our fuel cells recharged. A special grace seems to rest upon people with ongoing needs. You'll feel an overflow of that grace as you give away ministry to them.

Being around people with needs will also help you put your own problems in perspective. It will allow you avenues to connect with people that were previously closed.

Be aware—of compassion fatigue.

Galatians 6:9 says, "Let us not become weary in doing good, for at the proper time we will reap a harvest if we do not give up."

There is high turnover in ministry to the needy. This is the report we heard from the majority of ministries we talked with in doing research for this book. Burnout happens when people giving in ministry aren't nurtured.

Keeping Your Volunteers Motivated

If you're leading volunteers, be sure to let them know how valuable their service is. People choose to serve again—or not to—based on the experience they have each time. That means you have a chance to re-recruit someone every time he or she serves.

Have you prepared the supplies beforehand so that people don't waste time waiting? A volunteer may feel that inadequate planning on your part is disrespectful of his or her time. So think through all the needs of an outreach before the day arrives. Will you need tables, chairs, ice, transportation?

Take the lead in opening and closing the outreach with a short prayer. Monitor your volunteers regularly during the outreach to make sure they have what they need—including a planned restroom break and water to avoid dehydration.

Try to have a short debriefing meeting when you're finished with your project, if possible. Head out for pizza or some fast food after serving together. Ask people to share praise reports and any good things God did that day. Take notes on how to improve effectiveness for next time. Listen to the people. Both uneventful and stressful experiences can be redeemed as a person has a chance to share it with others.

Be a volunteer—for good!

Happy, fulfilled volunteers may tend to think wistfully and romantically about "going full time" into ministry to the needy. Urge them to reconsider. During my twenty years of full-time ministry, I (Steve) am proud to say that I've talked a lot of people out of going into the ministry. Believe me, it's not what it's cracked up to be. I've seen lives converted from fulfilled to distracted by turning from volunteer into full-time status. Consider the facts: People in full-time ministry work something like sixty hours per week. They're rarely thanked as volunteers are. They're severely underpaid for the amount of training and passion they possess. Their home lives often suffer.

Bottom line—only go into full-time ministry if it's absolutely the only option for you emotionally and spiritually, and then only after you have thoroughly, deeply prayed and consulted about such a drastic move.

STARTING A MINISTRY TO THE NEEDY

Pray

Ask God to show you the city as he sees the city. Ask for fresh eyes and a fresh perspective.

Look

. . . for the needs the Lord places in your path.

Interview

Check out people you're considering working with. You certainly don't need to jump into a ministry affiliation before you are ready. Take your time and mull over your options.

Experiment

Try on several ministries for size. See which one fits the best.

Just Start

Perhaps your "team" will initially consist of just you and one friend you bribe with the promise of pizza. That's fine as long as you're safe and not utterly overwhelmed in the process. Remember the saying of Uncle Steve (that's me): "There's nothing better for getting started than getting started."

"Focalize"

This is a special word. It's actually in the dictionary, but has been recently popularized by a new paraphrased version of the gospel of Mark entitled *The Hippie Bible and Commentary.* (To see "focalizing" in action, go to *The Hippie Bible* at www.logoschristian.org/mark and read Mark 1:3.) It's a great word that captures several ideas:

- To tell your vision
- To focus your attention
- To talk something up

When you are focalizing about your new ministry to the needy with great passion, people will listen. If you're getting your point across, they'll want to join you.

Tell Your Stories

We know we said this already. A little repetition doesn't hurt.

Your stories will help tremendously in the gathering together of a team. The most exciting and vibrant ministries to the needy in the coming years will rise up from the ranks of the volunteers who, right now, don't consider themselves all that knowledgeable on the topic. That's okay.

Take the Plunge
When you've come down to being involved in one ministry to people with needs, don't be overly cautious. Jump in. Give it at least six months to see how things are going before you take the apparent results very seriously. Remember: growth among ministries to the needy is sometimes a slow process.

Creatively Finance
Instead of asking the perhaps already-strapped, financially burdened local church to fund the start-up of your ministry to the needy, consider going to local business leaders for help.

If you can show them a clear plan, they'll be very likely to listen and respond.

You will likely also find in them a lending hand when it comes to manpower and materials. Many businesses are looking for creative ways to get involved in the community.

HURDLING OBSTACLES TO GETTING STARTED
It's simple to start serving people with needs—so simple that you might stumble over it. Feeling called is not the main requirement; being available is. Set this book down for a moment, grab a pen and paper, and take a note on this

"The great thing about serving the poor is that there is no competition."
—EUGENE RIVERS

next sentence so you don't miss it—it's that important. Ready? *Just get started!*

Let me repeat that: *Just get started!*

"There are so many needs—I don't know where to start."
That's fine. We didn't know where to start for the longest time. We've read a lot of books on ministry to the needy, and so far they've all contained the same story: No one has ever known what they were doing until they did it. By reading this section of this little book, you are literally better equipped to do ministry to the needy than most people are when they first start.

When we began to care for people with needs, we did it all wrong. Essentially everything we did was politically incorrect. We look back now and think that we couldn't have done things more poorly! But it still worked because we *did* meet people's needs.

"But we don't have any training."
You're getting some practical training now by reading this book. But it really doesn't take much training to begin to effectively reach out to the needy. It takes no expertise to minister to this group of the most resilient of all people.

After going out faithfully every Saturday morning for three years, several on our core team went out for pizza and a time of reflection on what we'd learned. When we began to recall how poorly we'd managed our "ministry" to the needy, we laughed until we cried. At times we just cried in embarrassment over how poorly we had represented the Lord in our outings. But through it all, we had sincerely tried to show people God's love. We had been *faithful*. And I now realize that faithfulness counts for a lot when it comes to outreach. We believe that nearly any approach to outreach to people with needs will work if you simply keep at it in faithfulness, because God rewards those who faithfully seek him.

"We don't have any resources."
Some of the projects in this book do need equipment. This might require organization and purchasing. However, you might be surprised at how eager other people will be to help care for the needy. In my experience, it's generally not difficult to raise money to minister to them. Put the word out—go to people and tell your story. Before you know it, you'll have the resources you need.

"I'm willing, but I can't lead the way all by myself."
People are attracted to a vision. They will rally around you as you take action to care for the needy. In fact, you may discover new leaders in your church among those who step out to minister to people with needs in your community. For years our main source of new leaders in ministries throughout the church initially were involved in our ministry to needy people.

Serve in teams of two or more for safety's sake. You'll also benefit from doing ministry in teams; synergy and energy come from serving together and sharing stories and observations afterward.

If you feel like you're failing, don't worry! The needy are very forgiving. The path to success goes right through failure. You'll find that people are resilient and willing to embrace you even in your most feeble attempts to minister to them. As long as you have the attitude of a learner and treat people with respect, dignity, and kindness, you will grow forward.

"How do I get a vision to start?"
Take a look at the original call given to the church at its inception. This is the Magna Carta of the kingdom of God that Jesus issued to the church as he launched his earthly ministry. When asked why he had come to the earth, he quoted from Isaiah chapter 61 the following words:

> "The Spirit of the Lord is on me, because he has anointed me to preach good news to the poor. He has sent me to proclaim freedom for the prisoners and recovery of sight for the blind, to release the oppressed, to proclaim the year of the Lord's favor." (Luke 4:18-19)

This book is organized around the four components of Jesus' words in the passage above:

1. Relief—"to release the oppressed"
   Giving care to an immediate problem, but not focusing on bringing a long-term solution to what's causing the problem.

2. Reconciliation—"to preach good news to the poor"
   Helping people get right with God and with one another.

3. Reconstruction—"to proclaim freedom for the prisoners"
   Working toward the creation of new economic opportunity.

You neutralize poverty "by keeping the focus on the characteristics of poor people rather than on the economy, politics, and society more broadly construed."[10]
   —ALICE O'CONNOR

4. Relocation—"he has sent me"
   Moving our physical location in order to bring the kingdom of God to people who need it.

LEVEL 1
RELIEF—MEETING AN IMMEDIATE NEED

IN SPITE OF SOME of the failures we've shared in the opening pages of this book, your outreach to people in need can have good beginnings, proper first steps. So this section—which makes up a good portion of this book—includes projects that will help you and your team get started. These are great courage builders before you take the next steps.

One way to think about the projects at this level is that they're like putting a bandage on an open wound. You may not cure any huge problems, but you will bring immediate relief to people with needs.

Most biblical exhortations to serve the needy center on this kind of immediate, relief-oriented work. As someone has said, "Find a hurt and heal it; find a need and meet it." It's Matthew 25 put into action:

> "I was hungry and you gave me something to eat, I was thirsty and you gave me something to drink, I was a stranger and you invited me in, I needed clothes and you clothed me, I was sick and you looked after me, I was in prison and you came to visit me." (Matthew 25:35-36)

It's not good to give in to the American tendency of desiring to "fix the system" at all costs. People around you might begin to think that by giving relief you're just throwing money and energy down a black hole. Again, the Bible doesn't have that perspective. Not every problem is fixable. You're not necessarily called to be the healers of every problem you encounter. You will be meeting the needs of many people along the way. On top of that, your relief work will be an enthusiasm-building activity.

1 NAIL CARE

Provide some special pampering with this outreach along with a great chance to connect in a significant way with the people you're serving. As you trim and file nails and apply polish in a hundred different shades, you'll make women and girls feel special. You'll spend time with them, give them undivided attention, and listen. And you'll probably end up praying for them. Something about all of that is refreshing to both body and soul. Many of them, particularly the children, haven't received much positive attention in their lives. You'll be a breath of fresh air.

WHAT YOU'LL NEED

- ☐ Cotton balls
- ☐ Nail polish remover
- ☐ Nail clippers
- ☐ Emory boards
- ☐ Variety of nail polishes
- ☐ Basket for supplies
- ☐ Trash bags
- ☐ Anti-bacterial wipes
- ☐ Hand lotion
- ☐ Cuticle softener
- ☐ Connection cards
  (see sample below)

How do you find people who can use nail care?
Set up where a crowd of people naturally gathers in an urban area. This is a good "companion" project, one that can be done in conjunction with another project listed in this book.

Connection Cards

When doing a project, it's important to have a means of connecting with those you serve. A connection card is a small, business-sized card you can leave with those you've served so they can get back in touch with you if they desire. The idea isn't to accomplish a sales job where you promote your church. Rather, it's a simple way to leave your church's name, address, phone number, and service times so that when future needs arise, those you've served will have a way of reconnecting with you. Certainly, more needs will crop up in the weeks and months to come, so it's crucial to leave some means of reconnection. The idea is to be available without giving out personal addresses.

Freshen-up on a hot summer day!

We hope this small gift brightens your day. It's a simple way of saying that God loves you—no strings attached. Let us know if we can be of more assistance.

v¹ney

1391 E. C
phone: 5
(147)

N

---

2 BREAD GIVEAWAY

Everyone likes bread, especially the high-end kind that is sold at stores that typically have "Bread Company" in their names (there are several assorted chains like this across the country). You can arrange to receive day-old bread from these classy bread stores for free! You can also check with national chain grocery stores that have in-house bakeries. Talk to the store manager and explain your outreach concept. Tell a few stories of the people you're helping and you'll likely establish your "daily bread connection." It

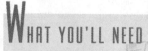

WHAT YOU'LL NEED

□ A supply of high-quality bread
□ Connection cards

will only take one or two of these connections to begin a substantial ministry to your community.

Many of these stores don't have a reliable source to distribute their old bread to. The key is to be consistent and reliable in picking up the bread. You'll need to have a team and a schedule so you don't disappoint the bread store managers. As a good public relations gesture, write a letter of thanks to the store manager for his company's generosity to the community (and don't be surprised to see it framed and posted on the wall of the store).

The ministry is simple and straightforward. Knock on the doors of houses or apartments. Say, "Hi, we're giving away free, fresh, high-quality bread. Could you use some or do you know anyone in the neighborhood who could use some?" Give recipients a connection card and offer to pray for them as you hand out the bread.

How do you find people to give bread to?
Cold calling (just knocking on doors) in lower-income neighborhoods and apartment complexes works fine with this project. Stay away from neighborhoods closest to the donating store.

3 DONUTS, COFFEE, AND CONVERSATION

Coffee and donuts together are a natural people and conversation magnet. This project works well among urban people in open spaces like parks. If you want to make this project work wonderfully well, give away the best donuts available. You'll then be making a statement to the community: "We *really* care about you!"

☐ Donuts
☐ Coffee
☐ Cream
☐ Sugar
☐ Artificial sweetener
☐ Cups
☐ Stir sticks
☐ Napkins
☐ Connection cards

You'll be putting your money where their mouths are.

In our community, for example, people consider Krispy Kreme donuts the best. As soon as the people we're ministering to see these, smiles abound, and the conversation takes off because we've demonstrated that we're friends!

Coffee backpacks work well with this project if you are doing any sizeable outreach. These specially designed contraptions are handy and available at our website, www.servantevangelism.com. Or you can pick up a caterer's coffee container, which holds five gallons of hot liquid, for about 120 dollars at a restaurant supply store.

Learn to ask good questions. Don't just get quiet while others are speaking. There's a big difference between quietness and listening. Get some listening training.

How do you find people to connect with by serving coffee and donuts?
Go to parks where a lot of people hang out on weekends. Retirement homes are good places as well, but get permission from the staff in advance. Housing shelters also work well for this outreach.

4 ID BADGES FOR THE HOMELESS

Keeping an identification card can be a daily issue for homeless people. But it's easy for them to misplace or to have their IDs stolen.

☐ Laptop computer
☐ Digital camera
☐ Portable color printer
☐ Simple graphics software
☐ Laminating machine
☐ Lariats
☐ Connection cards

Step out with an outreach to create IDs for all the homeless in your area.

This ID should include a clear photo of the person's face, his or her social security number (optional), Medicaid number, any special medical needs, and a name and phone number to contact in case of an emergency. An inexpensive way to produce these is to simply laminate the entire card. You can provide a wallet to keep this card in, or attach the card to a lariat to wear around the neck.

Regarding the supplies you need: Take the photo and print it on the spot with a battery-operated color printer. (Our team uses a Canon BJC 85 that costs about three hundred dollars; on a single battery it prints about one hundred sheets of 8x10s.) For software, you don't need anything as exotic as PhotoShop. Someone in your group may have a simple graphics program already loaded on their setup. It's probably the same person who has the digital camera and/or computer. A laminating machine for covering the finished card costs about two hundred dollars; you'll then spend approximately fifty cents per 2x3-inch badge. The laminator will require an AC power outlet. Radio Shack and other electronics stores sell converters for the DC outlet in your car (the cigarette lighter) for about one hundred dollars. Lariats for hanging the card around the neck cost twenty-five to fifty cents each.

For a less professional but quicker solution to all of the above, I-Zone Polaroid cameras take postage-stamp-sized color pictures. You need to get very close to the subject (eighteen inches away).

How do you find people who could use an ID badge?
Connect with those who run shelter housing as a starting point. The Salvation Army will also know who to direct you to. Or you can approach people "cold turkey" in parks if you're bold enough.

5 BACKPACKS FOR THE HOMELESS

Homeless people prefer backpacks for storing and transporting their possessions. They especially like the type of backpacks with bungee cords attached so they can tuck other things onto the outside of the packs.

These packs can actually be found on the Internet for as little as five dollars when purchased in quantity. Instead of just providing people with an empty pack, fill it with some of life's essentials, such as a toothbrush, toothpaste, a comb, a brush, deodorant, and nail clippers.

W HAT YOU'LL NEED

- ☐ Backpacks
- ☐ Backpack contents (toothbrush, comb, and so on)
- ☐ Connection cards (laminated for protection against rough handling and moisture)

How do you find people to give backpacks to?
Give these out at other events that attract homeless people (such as the coffee and donuts giveaway). You can also connect with the homeless through a local shelter.

6 BACKPACKS FILLED WITH SCHOOL SUPPLIES

Some children fall into a pattern of chronic absenteeism early in the school year because their parents can't afford required school supplies. Give students a leg up by sending them back to school with supplies they'll need and you'll help them feel confident going into the year.

WHAT YOU'LL NEED

□ Backpacks
□ School supplies
□ Connection cards

School backpacks can be purchased for about seven dollars each in quantity on the Internet. Fill the packs with school supplies. Supplies vary by district and grade level, so call local school systems to ask what is specifically needed for each grade. In addition, many large discount stores and office supply stores offer copies of school supply lists. Remember that these lists differ from school to school and grade to grade. "Load" the packs according to grade and school system and label them before they're distributed.

How do you find kids to give backpacks to?
Most local school districts will provide names of families who can use help with school supplies. The Salvation Army is also a good source.

7 YELLOW BAG GROCERY COLLECTION AT CHURCH

As people leave your church services, hand them bright yellow plastic bags (which can be purchased from American Paper and Plastic at 1-800-822-5600) with a card listing five to ten food items. The next week, families bring the bags back filled with food and leave them behind their cars. Teams drive around the parking lot and pick up the donations during that week's service(s)—quick in, quick out.

WHAT YOU'LL NEED

□ Yellow bags
□ Cards listing suggested food items

How do you find people to collect food from?
Your church! They will be eager to participate once they get the vision of what the food will be used for.

8 TIPPING FAST-FOOD WORKERS

Many of the adults working in the fast-food industry are from among the ranks of the working poor. An unexpected dollar or two as a tip is tremendously appreciated. Unfortunately, Christians have a reputation for being bad tippers. You can immediately change that perception by tipping fast-food workers, who typically receive no tips.

WHAT YOU'LL NEED

□ Special connection cards

Leave special connection cards that include an additional line: "Here's a little something extra. We hope this brought some light into your day. If we can be of more help, please give us a call."

How do you find people to tip?
Approach workers at fast-food restaurants. Also under-tipped are housecleaning staff at hotels and motels.

IN ACTION: Seacoast Community Church in Charleston, South Carolina, issued a challenge to their church members. They put their heads together and came up with a tipping campaign that swept through the city and put their church's name on the map. They offer preprinted cards for members to leave only if they commit to giving a great tip above and beyond the usual 15 to 20 percent. And they tip in unexpected places, such as fast-food restaurants, where workers can especially use the money. Now the city is buzzing with excitement, and other churches have caught on to the tipping craze. They're reversing the trend one food worker observed: "The longer the prayer for the food, the smaller the tip."

9 CLEANING UP A NEIGHBORHOOD

The work that needs to be done in many urban neighborhoods seems to be without end. It's sometimes a question of "Where do we get started that's going to make any difference?"

WHAT YOU'LL NEED

- ☐ Clean-up tools
- ☐ Rakes
- ☐ Brooms
- ☐ Garbage bags
- ☐ Connection cards

The key to working with an inner-city neighborhood is to be helpful, but not to come across as patronizing to residents. You'll find it vital to work hand in hand with neighborhood leaders. Plan projects with leaders whom residents look up to and you'll change the perception of the project from a handout to a hand up.

For some inspiring stories of people who have done some great urban renewal projects, check with the Soul Survivor folks in Great Britain (www.soulsurvivor.com).

How do you find people who need their neighborhood cleaned up?

Ask around in neighborhoods with older residents who could use help with their dwellings. They're usually a safe place to start. Once you've gotten your feet wet, begin to contact urban leaders of other neighborhoods and begin to build relationships for future outreaches.

10 DOOR TO DOOR WITH BAGS OF FOOD

Nothing says love like a bag full of food. This is perhaps the simplest approach to ministry to the needy. You simply knock on doors and say, "Hi, I'm ____. We have food for anyone who can use it. If you need any, or if anyone else in the neighborhood does, we can help!"

WHAT YOU'LL NEED

- ☐ Bags
- ☐ Nonperishable food
- ☐ Connection cards

As with all projects, go out in teams of two or more. After you've given out a bag of groceries, it's quite natural to offer to pray for the individual or family that you're serving. Be open to hearing from God.

How do you find people to serve with bags of food?

You can go to whomever you meet in this door-to-door fashion, or you can go to specific shut-ins or families that you know who are in need.

11 HAIR CARE

Most people need haircuts in order to feel good about themselves. While washing is usually impractical, you can creatively do hair care apart from that. Set up cutting and styling stations in parks. Because cutting the hair of different people groups is unique, you'll need to bring appropriate equipment and personnel for the people you will serve. Disinfect combs and brushes between clients. Girls will feel special with braids, French braiding, assorted ponytails, scrunchies, ribbons, barrettes, and clips in their hair. Don't forget to give them hugs and praise freely!

Once you get a consistent team going, this ministry can be repeated on an every-other-month basis—same time, same place, same people.

WHAT YOU'LL NEED

- ☐ Cutting equipment
- ☐ Ribbons
- ☐ Combs
- ☐ Disinfectant
- ☐ People to cut hair
- ☐ Power cords
- ☐ Power strips
- ☐ Mirrors
- ☐ Connection cards

How do you find people who need hair care?
Look for them among those gathered in a park, staying at a shelter, or connected with a Salvation Army facility. Distribute flyers a few days before to announce the event, and include the date as well as beginning and ending times.

12 COLORING WITH CHILDREN

You mean just coloring with children? Yes! This is one of the simplest yet most profound projects of the 101. We have found it very effective for connecting with families—children and their parents alike.

With this project, as with all outreaches involving children, you need to make sure that all adults are

- • *Totally safe.* Consider doing a legal screen of all participants. A background check will cost a bit of money but will be well

WHAT YOU'LL NEED

- ☐ Crayons
- ☐ Edifying and biblical coloring sheets
- ☐ Candies or toys for prizes

worth the investment for the peace of mind it will bring to your outreach. Someone connected with law enforcement can direct you through the particulars involved with getting background checks done.

- *Team players.* Minister to children in settings where two or more adults are present. It just makes sense.
- *Living in the light.* Do all ministry in the open—never behind a closed door. You don't want to have the appearance of any evil at any time.

How do you find kids to color with?
This is a great project to do in conjunction with one of the other projects that ministers to parents.

You can also simply knock on doors and do the "pied piper" drill—tell parents that your team is holding a coloring contest. Create a lot of categories for winners so that *no one* leaves without a small prize. As some team members are ministering to the children, have another crew connecting with the parents.

13 CLOTHES TO GO

Remember this axiom: Clothes are always popular! It's true. Giving away clothes is always in season, no matter what part of the city you're located in. People are always looking for good, stylish, new-to-them clothes.

You may find that it's better not to *give* clothes away for free. Sometimes the "free" encourages hoarding. Instead, sell them for next to nothing—something like a nickel per item.

A clothing ministry is easy to start. Once you issue a call for used clothing, you'll have plenty! But while it's easy to get clothes, getting *good* clothes can be a more difficult matter. Sometimes people give junk that they haven't worn in ten years, and certainly no one else in his or her right mind would ever wear those items either.

So specify that you want good, in-season, used clothes that are

WHAT YOU'LL NEED

- ☐ System for gathering clothes
- ☐ System for sorting
- ☐ Hangers
- ☐ Measuring tape
- ☐ Masking tape to mark sizes

currently in fashion. You're looking for items that people would still wear—maybe the clothes just don't fit or the color isn't right. Having said that, we suggest that you go ahead and receive anything that comes in as a donation. People have a need to give—it's good for the soul. Call a thrift store such as those run by Goodwill, the Salvation Army, or another charity to pick up extra clothes you can't give away.

Emphasize that you can always use winter coats. When cold weather hits, you won't be able to keep enough of them in stock to meet the demand.

How do you find people who need clothes?
They're everywhere! As you let the word out, those in need of clothing will show up and stand in line to receive good used clothing. This project works well alone but it also works well in conjunction with most of the other projects listed in this book.

Recycle Prom or Bridesmaid Dresses

If you have no way to find a recipient for that dress you'll never wear again but hate to throw away, visit www.glassslipperproject.org to donate it to needy teens in Chicago or other areas around the country. Check in the website under How You Can Help then Out-of-state information.

14 DOOR-TO-DOOR GIVEAWAYS

You can give away just about anything to show God's love in a practical way. For a great starter list, read some of the simple outreach projects in *101 Ways to Reach Your Community* (NavPress, 2001). In inner-city neighborhoods, you'll find myriad needs on any given day. You can intersect people's lives in everyday ways by simply knocking on their doors and saying, "Hi, I'm _____, and we're showing God's love in a practical way by giving away _____ today. Could you use any?"

The gifts vary from candy, to soft drinks, to rolls of paper towels, toilet paper, light bulbs, batteries—you name it. If it's practical, it will probably work. The general idea is to show them God's love, not just talk about it. There are so

WHAT YOU'LL NEED

☐ Things to give away
☐ Connection cards

many practical ways to demonstrate God's love, you could return to the same homes week after week with different gifts. The recipients will eventually ask you why you're being so nice. This is a great application of the verse "Always be prepared to give an answer to everyone who asks you to give the reason for the hope that you have" (1 Peter 3:15).

How do you find people who need things?
Just go door to door, knock, and start talking to strangers. You'll meet the nicest people when giving things for free!

15 PASS IT ON—COMPUTERS

Computers now last about two years before they need to be replaced (forget about the term "upgrade"—that's been retired!).

WHAT YOU'LL NEED

□ System for collecting computers
□ System for cleaning up computers
□ Inexpensive or donated software
□ Computer refurbishers

But instead of throwing them in a landfill, implement this project. You can take these still-useful computers and make sure they're operational. Clean any unsuitable materials off the hard drives, then give them to students or families in need of a viable computer to use or to learn computer skills with.

You can also give used computers to many churches, schools, and after-school programs in lower-income neighborhoods. The Full Circle Group in Cincinnati (www.full-circlegroup.org)—which is manned by volunteers who are computer professionals, hobbyists, educators, network specialists, students, and retirees—recycles more than one thousand computers a year. You can find another group at www.cristina.org that will recycle donations of PCs that are 486 or better to give to needy folks.

Along with a Pass It On—Computers program, you can offer basic training in word processing, spreadsheet, and e-mail and web browsing programs to round out the user's skill set (see project 88). This will help users hit the ground running in the computer universe and perhaps even in the job market.

The Pass It On—Computers program is a good deal for all involved. The giver receives a tax credit for the equipment donated. The needy receive a much-needed computer. And skilled volunteers can share their knowledge.

Put the word out modestly on this ministry and you will be

surprised at the number of computers coming your direction. We predict as many as you can handle!

How do you find people who could most benefit from computers? Connect with people who are already coming to other ministries such as a pantry or clothing ministry—people you see repeatedly and have a good idea that they have an authentic need. Contact the Salvation Army to see who they recommend for this ministry.

Or connect with a local shelter. Instead of giving the computer, set up several computers with software and begin to teach computer and software skills to the shelter residents.

16 PASS IT ON—EYEGLASSES

Eyeglasses are expensive and out of economic reach for many in need. On the other hand, others who wear glasses have more pairs than they can keep track of. You can collect good, reasonably fashionable, used glasses and reissue them to those in need. The used glasses need to be "sized" for the strength of their lenses, but this can be done by a volunteer optometrist or optometric assistant with a machine that measures lens strength. Mark the right lens and left lens strength, then slip the pair of glasses in a cardboard case and file it for future use.

To distribute the glasses, do a simple eye test similar to what your school nurse did in elementary school—one eye covered at a time at a set distance. This simple test can be given by volunteer optometrists or by trained lay volunteers.

After testing, fit people for glasses, and they'll leave being able to see clearly. There's nothing like a pleased, seeing customer with a big smile on his or her face.

How do you get eyeglasses for use in this outreach?

WHAT YOU'LL NEED
- ☐ Glasses that are sized
- ☐ Testing equipment
- ☐ Trained testers

Many professionals who work for eyeglass manufacturers are very generous and interested in community involvement. Try national chain eyeglass manufacturers. In addition, begin a used glasses campaign.

How do you find people who could benefit from eyeglasses?
Offer eyeglasses in addition to another ministry you sponsor, such

as at a big party (see project 51). Inquire at your local homeless shelter.

Want to donate glasses for others to give away to someone in need?
The Lions Club collects eyeglasses and sunglasses for people in developing countries. Drop off old pairs at a Lions Club center (call 1-800-74-SIGHT for a location) or at any LensCrafters store.

17 SAMARITAN RUNS

There's nothing like a Samaritan Run for a great get-your-feet-wet project to needy people. This is designed to bring out the Good Samaritan in each of us (there's one lurking there somewhere!).

WHAT YOU'LL NEED

☐ Food
☐ Shoes
☐ Coats
☐ Blood pressure cuffs
☐ Children's games
☐ Folding tables and chairs
☐ Transportation
☐ Connection cards

On Saturday mornings (When else is everyone off work?), head out for no more than two hours. Outreaches that last longer become arduous and lose volunteers. Go out in fairly large groups—it's just plain fun to go with a bunch of people, and you'll always find safety in numbers. After praying on site, go into the specific project.

You can offer a number of outreach projects at a Samaritan Run:

- Screening for blood pressure
- Distributing shoes
- Giving away coats in the winter
- Feeding peanut butter and jelly sandwiches and Kool-Aid
- Listening
- Playing with children

After a short time, a beehive of activity will be happening, and the two hours go by amazingly quickly. All those who come out to minister will be encouraged when they see that God will use them no matter how small the project they get involved with. They see that God can use them to do special things in ministry.

The Samaritan Run can serve as a springboard for a number of other ministries to the needy, as participants come up with creative ideas and step out in boldness.

How do you find people to come to your Samaritan Runs?
We usually go to parks where people are hanging out. When the weather is inclement, we go to homeless shelters.

IN ACTION: Blood-N-Fire Ministries (www.bloodnfire.com) in Atlanta, Georgia, is a radical church that was started to serve the poor. They admit that when they started, they didn't have a clue what they were doing when it came to ministry to the poor. They took a few bags of groceries to some projects in a rather dangerous part of town and began to knock on doors. A dozen years later, something very unusual is going on. They purchased an old cotton mill and rehabbed it into a meeting place that doubles as a shelter for a couple hundred homeless people involved in their school of discipleship. It's run by volunteers who raise their own support to work there. A healthy cross section of needy people and suburbanites of Greater Atlanta who have a heart for the poor attend the services there.

18 WALKMANS WITH CASSETTES FOR STREET PEOPLE

This project gives hope and keeps on giving long after the initial gift! Give out Walkman-style cassette players along with a tape specifically made for those who are in need of hope. Have someone make a ministry of compiling the tapes, with Scripture verses mixed with soft music in the background. For a street person, this can be a tremendous gift that brings hope for months to come.

WHAT YOU'LL NEED

□ Low-priced cassette Walkmans
□ Tapes
□ Batteries
□ Connection cards

Before you conclude that this project is too expensive, consider this: Walkman-style cassette players with simple headphones can be purchased now for as little as seven dollars (on the Internet). Prerecorded cassettes are available for less than a dollar at our website (www.servantevangelism.com), or call toll free at 1-888-KINDNESS (see project 23 for details).

Because the players will need new batteries occasionally, you'll have a great reason to connect with street people. When you reconnect, you can also offer them a new Scripture music tape.

How do you find people to give Walkmans and Scripture tapes to? Connect with street people, the homeless in your community (check with law enforcement officers), and people living in shelters.

19 ADOPT A PRISONER

The idea of ministering to people in prison as Jesus directed in Matthew 25 doesn't sound all that safe for most people—at least when you consider caring for a prisoner on a one-to-one basis. We have known several women who, with all good intentions, attempted to visit or write to prisoners and ended up being harassed for years after their well-intentioned act. But if you "adopt" a prisoner as a group, you'll experience significantly greater safety.

WHAT YOU'LL NEED

☐ Agreement between your group and the prisoner

Include a visit as a group on or near the holidays and on the prisoner's birthday. You might well be the only people visiting him or her. When you start this ministry, be sure to clearly spell out the kind of relationship you will have with the prisoner. Also, be clear that if he or she violates the agreement once, there will be a warning. A second violation of established boundaries will mean ending the relationship.

Bless a Prisoner with Books

Recycle your good used paperbacks. Books To Prisoners sends books to inmates who request them. Mail paperbacks fourth class to Books To Prisoners, c/o Left Bank Books, Box A, 92 Pike Street, Seattle, WA 98101. And check them out at their web address: http://btp.tao.ca/.

How do you find a prisoner to adopt?
Contact a local prison or jail chaplain. Explain what you're hoping to do. Ask for recommendations of several inmates, for their names and photos, if possible, and for brief histories on each (if the prisoner agrees to release that information) for adoption purposes.

20 ADOPT A PRISONER'S FAMILY

A small group that is focused only inward is ultimately an unhealthy small group. Break out of a rut by adopting the family of an inmate. As a group you can become a mentoring force for a family in need.

Include this family in your group outings, such as picnics, movies, or trips to local museums. Invite the family to holiday activities and other events at your church. At Christmas provide gifts, dinner, and tree trimmings for the family. Consider the

WHAT YOU'LL NEED

☐ Agreement between your group and the prisoner's family

children's needs throughout the school year and look for ways to help, such as providing school supplies, buying shoes, or connecting the family with the school lunch program. The spouse of the imprisoned might even become an active part of your small group.

How do you find a prisoner's family to adopt?
Contact a local chaplain. Explain your vision for the adopt-a-family project. Ask for recommendations of several inmates' families, for their names, and for photos if possible. If the prisoner would agree to release the information, you can also ask to review a brief history for group adoption purposes. Often a good chaplain will have information on prisoners' families as he or she provides care for them.

Note: Before adopting a family, pray about the specific family you're about to choose. Openly discuss your options as a group. You'll have to live with this choice for a long time—perhaps even after the family member who's in prison is released.

Once you make your choice, invite the family over for a social time to break the ice. Purchase a small gift for each family member as a way of saying, "We love you and we want to get involved in your life!"

21 THANKSGIVING DINNER

Jesus said, "Go out to the roads and country lanes and make them come in, so that my house will be full" (Luke 14:23). With this verse in mind, consider inviting needy people to your home for Thanksgiving instead of eating it with your family alone. You

WHAT YOU'LL NEED

- Food
- Plates and silverware (not paper plates)
- Name tags or place cards

might be surprised—the idea might well catch on and become the highlight of your family holiday.

Unlike Christmas, where events can be difficult to get people excited about because of time conflicts, Thanksgiving is a great time for an outreach.

How do you find an individual or family to adopt at Thanksgiving?

If your church runs a food pantry, this is a natural extension of that ministry. Invite people to join you from among those who use the pantry. You can also invite shut-ins or the elderly from your community. People with disabilities are often forgotten on holidays like Thanksgiving, but you can usually find them by asking at county welfare offices.

22 GIVEAWAY BAGS TO COLLECT FOOD

WHAT YOU'LL NEED

- Yellow plastic bags
- List of suggested food items
- Connection cards or letters

Wealthier folks have a need to give to the needy, but they might not really know how to take action.

Leave a bright yellow bag (one source for these bags is American Paper and Plastic at 1-800-822-5600) on the doorknobs of suburban homes. Include a preprinted flyer with the following explanation:

Hi,

We are holding a party for people in need! We'll be giving away a lot of food and clothing and generally having a great time for all who attend.

Many people are giving a few food items to our project. We'll collect food left in this yellow bag next Saturday between 10 and noon. Attached are some food items that would work well for this food giveaway. Or simply donate any nonperishable food items you'd like to.

Thanks so much for your generosity! If you have

any questions about this project, please call us at
_____.

SINCERELY,

_____ CHURCH

SPONSORING CHURCH

P.S. The party will be held on (date) from (time beginning to ending) at (location). Feel free to stop by!

How do you find people who will give you food at the door?
Garden-variety suburbanites will respond well to this outreach.

23 CDS AND CASSETTES

Giving free worship music and recorded Scripture is a great way to begin your connection with needy families. Purchase and distribute worship music that is appropriate to your audience. Or, better, record your own worship tunes. If you have an ample supply of non-copyrighted songs, consider mixing those with recorded Scripture.

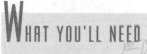

WHAT YOU'LL NEED

☐ Tapes or CDs
☐ Connection cards

Steven B. Stevens, who has one of the most familiar voices in Scripture recording today, has worked out a deal with our church in Cincinnati to do a series of Scripture promise tapes. These are non-copyrighted tapes, so you can purchase these and use them as they are, or you can mix in your own music with the Scripture for a great gift to families in needy neighborhoods. We recommend you also add a section at the end of your tapes with information about your church, such as meeting times, location, and phone number.

Tapes from us cost less than one dollar (at the time of this printing) and are available at either our website (www.servant-evangelism.com) or by calling toll free at 1-888-KINDNESS. These tapes are available on a number of topics.

How do you find people to give CDs and cassettes to?
Simply go door to door with the tapes. Knock on doors cold turkey and offer the tapes, saying that you're showing God's love in a practical way.

24 COMPASSION WEEKEND

Launch a whole set of compassion ministries in "one fell swoop" by holding a Compassion Weekend. This project exposes your people to a broad range of approaches to ministry to the needy. Run projects sponsored by your church throughout the weekend (Friday through Sunday). Invite small groups, families, and daring individuals to try new projects on their own. Create a feedback form for participants to complete when they're all done.

WHAT YOU'LL NEED

- ☐ Creative projects
- ☐ Enthusiastic leaders
- ☐ Supplies for the projects
- ☐ Connection cards

Give attention to the "most creative project," "most daring project," "did-the-most-with-the-least-amount project," "largest heart project." Celebrate the heart and heroism shown by the people.

Find your list of projects among those mentioned in this book.

How do you find people to serve on a Compassion Weekend?
The activists in your church will volunteer when you begin to promote it. Invite the shyer people in your congregation if you know they'll resonate with a particular outreach. If you're still concerned about enough people participating, hold the weekend in conjunction with another church in your area, or limit the time frame to Saturday morning from nine to noon. Be sure to make time for sharing "war stories" at your next gathering.

25 TAKE A BAG WITH A MAP AS YOU LEAVE

As families and single people leave church, offer them a bag of groceries on a rack by the door to deliver to a needy family or a shut-in. Provide an easy-to-read map from your church location to the residence of the person in need. The bags can include an assortment of what a family or individual would need for several meals. Leave some that don't include maps but with a note that says, "Deliver to someone you know to be in need."

WHAT YOU'LL NEED

- ☐ Bags of food
- ☐ Maps
- ☐ Connection cards

How do you find people to serve with "bags to go"?
Connect with social services in your area—they will give you plenty of needs. You can also find out when government assistance checks are issued in your area. Families on public assistance typically run short of food a few days before the next checks arrive.

26 POTLUCK IN THE PARK

All churches have potlucks. Some of the best memories many people have of growing up in a church are connected with times of fellowship around food, laughter, and conversation. This project takes that event and turns it inside out. Instead of having an insiders' potluck, everyone brings twice as much to a city park to share with people.

Before the event, one team needs to arrive about forty-five minutes early to invite people in the neighborhood to the event by going door to door with printed flyers. At the same time, another group decorates tables in the park with colorful plastic or paper tablecloths.

WHAT YOU'LL NEED

☐ Classic potluck food
☐ Entertainment for kids
☐ Decorations
☐ Paper products
☐ Games
☐ Prizes
☐ A team for inviting
☐ A team for set up and serving
☐ A team for cleanup
☐ Flyers with times and location

All of your hard work will be for nothing unless you keep in mind a key word: mingle! Hang out with your guests. Don't spend time with the people you already know. Even though that will be comfortable for you, nothing will make your guests feel more *un*comfortable.

How do you find people to attend a potluck in the park?
Simply knock on doors and invite people.

27 CAFÉ RENT-OUT FOR BIRTHDAYS

Cheers was one of the most popular and beloved TV shows a few years ago because it was a place "where everybody knows your name." Everyone needs places like that in life—places of safety and belonging. Create a monthly place for a neighborhood to

WHAT YOU'LL NEED

- ☐ A cozy café
- ☐ Cake
- ☐ Punch
- ☐ Ice cream
- ☐ Party favors
- ☐ Balloons
- ☐ Party games
- ☐ Piñata
- ☐ Plates
- ☐ Cups
- ☐ Forks
- ☐ Spoons
- ☐ Napkins
- ☐ Gifts

belong—for the least, the lost, the lonely, and the forgotten to fit in.

Rent out a local café and throw a party for everyone who had a birthday during that given month. Invite the neighborhood and make this a community-building activity. To make it festive, have a piñata, cake and ice cream (a huge cake with "Happy Birthday to You" inscribed on it), party favors, and a gift for each of the neighborhood residents with birthdays.

How do you find people to invite to a Café Rent-Out?
Knock on doors in the neighborhood you are focusing on for your outreach. Connect with a homeless shelter for additional names.

28 SOCK OUTREACH

Homeless people need new socks frequently as they tend to wear out socks more quickly than most people. The socks of choice among homeless people are generally thick tube-style socks or walking socks with extra heel and toe support.

WHAT YOU'LL NEED

- ☐ A crew to find, buy, and sort socks
- ☐ Socks
- ☐ Connection cards

This is a great project for senior adults in your church to get involved in. They can take charge of gathering, sorting, and packaging. Some groups of senior church members might want to do it all—from advertising the need for socks, to sorting the donations, to distributing the packages to homeless people.

How do you find people to give socks to?
Check with the staff at homeless shelters, call your local Salvation Army chapter, or simply go to public parks where homeless people hang out.

29 TRANSPORTATION FOR THE WORKING NEEDY

The reason employers don't hire people with needs isn't that employers aren't willing to hire, but that there are many secondary issues connected with hiring people coming out of a poverty situation.[11] Whether it's due to a lack of social skills or something as simple as getting to work on time, these needy people often struggle with consistency.

WHAT YOU'LL NEED

□ A driver
□ A second person to navigate
□ Cargo van
□ Cell phone

Often they just need a little help to get moving forward, and transportation to and from work is a big issue for many. If you want to begin to make a difference and if you have adequate time and an available cargo van (such as a church van that's not in use on weekdays), you could start something great.

To get this ministry started you'll need to have a clear understanding between you and the people you're serving: for example, an agreement that they need to go to work every day, no matter what, for a given period of time—say ninety days.

Note: For safety's sake, a woman should not do this ministry alone.

How do you find people who need transportation?
Connect with those you already know through other ministries to the community.

30 "SOUPER BOWL"

Each year, the Christian Broadcasting Network sponsors a "Souper Bowl" event in the city where the Super Bowl is held. This mercy-oriented event, held a week prior to the NFL championship, is designed to specifically help the working needy.

WHAT YOU'LL NEED

□ Food
□ Games
□ Sports clinics
□ Used clothes
□ Connection cards

Tens of thousands of people show up for these festivities. You can do something similar on a smaller scale either on the day of the Super

LEVEL 1: RELIEF—MEETING AN IMMEDIATE NEED **51**

Bowl or during the week before the Super Bowl with the same format as the Souper Bowl. Consider having local college or professional sports figures who are Christians give their testimonies (plus they'll help draw crowds).

How do you find people who would benefit from a Souper Bowl?
Distribute flyers in advance. Advertise on local radio stations. If you approach station managers with your project's vision at least a month ahead of the event, you'll likely receive free radio time.

31 CHRISTMAS GIFT-GIVING SHOP

Many people in need can't afford to support their families and handle added expenses during the holidays. You can help by providing a free shopping spree, with each child receiving three presents chosen by his or her parents. Schedule the event to last about three hours, and consider holding it at a community center in the neighborhood you want to reach.

WHAT YOU'LL NEED

- ☐ Friendly, enthusiastic volunteers
- ☐ CD player and Christmas CDs
- ☐ Gifts to give away
- ☐ Toys to distribute
- ☐ Clothes to give away
- ☐ Connection cards

Place donated items on display as they would be in a store. Church members donate either new or gently used items. You'll be amazed at the number of decent gifts you can gather when everyone helps a little. In addition to presents, used clothing works very well if it's in great condition. If you're concerned about not having enough of a people pool to draw from—for example, if your church is too small to do this project alone—consider doing it with one or two other small churches as a cooperative project. There's even more fun in numbers!

This project can create quite a back-up because it takes time for each person to go through the queue and choose his or her presents. Appoint some friendly people to hand out flyers to those who are waiting. List other events you're holding during the holidays and after the New Year. Include other services you offer to people in this neighborhood, such as Kid's Clubs, Bible studies, and a Christmas party for the neighborhood—complete with an ethnically correct Santa.

How do you find people who would be interested in the Christmas gift-giving shop?
Connect with people through other projects you are doing. Also, check out Salvation Army connections.

You can also go to the local schools and ask principals which families seem to have the greatest needs. Or talk to apartment managers in low-income housing areas to get their cooperation, referrals, and even a community center or rec room to use.

32 TAX HELP

WHAT YOU'LL NEED

Though their taxes are fairly easy to calculate, many needy people don't fill out the forms and send in for refunds because no one guides them. Often they need just a little bit of help to fill out the paperwork and send in the federal and state forms.

☐ Trustworthy tax preparers
☐ Calculators
☐ Tax forms
☐ Stamps
☐ Current tax manual
☐ Pens
☐ Pencils
☐ Note pads
☐ Connection cards

Most have very few tax deductions to deal with, and calculations are straightforward. Most important is that the people helping be trustworthy and that this quality clearly comes across to those in need. Senior adults are ideal for this ministry.

How do you find people who need tax help?
Knock on doors or leave flyers advertising a Saturday morning event in a community room, in an apartment building, or in low-income housing projects. Also, connect with people you already know through other ministries to needy people.

33 TRASH PICKUP

WHAT YOU'LL NEED

Urban neighborhoods often have significant need for clean-up. As opposed to just making things look nicer, aim for picking up debris that's a health hazard: broken glass, needles, pieces of rough metal, nails, and so on. This is a good project to do at bus stops, parks, libraries, fast-food restaurants,

☐ Plastic bags
☐ Five-gallon buckets
☐ Rubber gloves
☐ "Pickup sticks" with nail points
☐ "Grabber" sticks for picking up gross trash
☐ Connection cards

or on sidewalks and in parking lots.

You can also hire homeless people to help pick up trash. Ask them what they think their time is worth—or give them a five-dollar bill for half an hour of work.

With this project it isn't necessary to talk to anyone. In fact, the lower key the better. You might want to wear vests or T-shirts printed with a message—something like "Kindness in Progress"—so that passersby know what you're up to.

How do you find people who need trash picked up?
Who doesn't need trash picked up? Just don't come across as patronizing to those you're helping.

34 ADOPT A BLOCK

Instead of a hit-or-miss approach to ministering to a neighborhood, consider going out consistently to the same neighborhood and planting seeds of kindness and mercy in a specific area. The adopt-a-block concept is tantamount to farming one particular field over and over.

WHAT YOU'LL NEED

☐ Eager, spiritually mature believers

What sorts of projects can be done? This book is full of them, or check out the previous book in this series, *101 Ways to Reach Your Community*. The idea is to "own" in an emotional sense a piece of geography and to come back to that area regularly.

How do you find people who would like to be a part of an adopt-a-block program?
A small group or an adult Sunday school class might own a block together in prayer and in support.

35 PRAYER-WALKING

Popularized by Steve Hawthorne and Graham Kendrick's book *Prayer-Walking* (Creation House, 1993), this is a very hands-on approach to praying for your ministry area. Rather than praying from afar, you put legs on your prayers and go out to the people. Pray and walk at the same time (pray in your head or under your breath).

As simple as it sounds—walking and praying for a neighborhood—seeking to get the heart and mind of God for an area is a very effective way to hear God when you're first getting started with a ministry to the needy.

You might try an alternative, such as driving around the perimeter of your community or riding bikes while praying. Another great place to pray is the local mall—the modern equivalent of the old town square.

WHAT YOU'LL NEED

☐ A bit of space in your schedule

How do you pray for a neighborhood?
Be intuitive. Pray the prayers God gives you to pray. Pray Scripture, agreeing with God and his purposes for this neighborhood or place.

36 VEGETABLE AND FRUIT GIVEAWAY

Everyone likes fresh corn, green beans, tomatoes, and watermelon in the summer—even kids who know it's politically incorrect to like their veggies. Stock up by buying a quantity of vegetables or fruit from a local grower or at a warehouse club.

WHAT YOU'LL NEED

☐ Fruit or vegetables
☐ Bags or baskets
☐ Connection cards

Go door to door with your gift and ask for the mother of the house. Don't leave the gift unless you hand it to an adult. Kids are usually forgetful.

Some giveaways that work well include:

• Pumpkins
• Watermelons
• Squash
• Apples
• Carrots
• Corn

How do you find people to give vegetables and fruit to?
Drive through the neighborhood you're ministering to with a portable PA system to announce the outreach: "Come and get free _____! We're just showing God's love in a practical way!"

37 COMMUNITY GARDENS

This project is less about putting vegetables on the tables of the needy and more about sowing seeds of relationships whose roots run so deep they last a lifetime. There's nothing like getting a little bit of dirt under one's fingernails and sharing some honest sweat to draw people together.

WHAT YOU'LL NEED

☐ Open area to "farm"
☐ Seeds
☐ Flowers
☐ Bean poles
☐ Hoses
☐ Watering source
☐ Shovels
☐ Gardening gloves
☐ Plant food

If you don't know much about gardening, don't worry. This outreach is not really about being an expert gardener. Pick up a copy of *The Complete Idiot's Guide to Gardening* (Macmillan, 1997) and you'll be on your way. Vegetables can be packed tightly together if you feed and water them enough. Also consider planting flowers for beautification. If you want to come back year after year, put in some perennial plants.

Remember, your goal is to do more than grow zucchini. The objective is to grow hearts together. This shared experience is the *community* in a community garden.

How do you find people to cooperatively do a community garden with?
Go door to door in neighborhoods to see who's interested in working in the garden and getting a share of the crops.

38 HEALTH SCREENINGS

This project involves screening for a number of health problems and could include different types of testing:

WHAT YOU'LL NEED

☐ Testing kits and equipment
☐ Connection cards

• Hearing
• Sight
• Blood pressure
• Cholesterol
• HIV
• STDs

Doctors do the majority of the tests, although trained volunteers can administer sight, hearing, and blood pressure tests. Connect with either the Salvation Army or a shelter ministry to provide the needed facilities for doing the examinations.

Some pharmaceutical companies may donate the screening kits and/or the lab work once they learn of your ministry; others may offer their services at a greatly discounted price.

You'll need an examining room or enclosed canopy—a different one for each screening center. Some of the tests will be taken that day and the results reported back later.

How do you find people who need a health screening?
Check out several sources: street preachers who know an area, low-income housing, apartment buildings, and senior citizen residences. Also, you can hit the streets and ask a "sideways" question, such as, "We're doing free health screenings for _____ and _____. Do you know anyone in the neighborhood who could use the help?"

Be aware: The concept of preventative medicine runs somewhat counter to life on the streets, where the approach is more often, "Go to the doctor as a last resort." Approach people with the idea, "Don't you want to have the peace of mind that there's nothing wrong with you?"

39 BUS TOKEN GIVEAWAY

Have you ridden a bus lately? The needy do it all the time, but it's not fun—many aspects are difficult, inconvenient, and even slightly dehumanizing. Head to busy bus stops and offer free bus tokens to riders as they wait. At the same time, distribute goodies such as granola bars, cookies,

WHAT YOU'LL NEED

☐ Bus tokens
☐ Food
☐ Bottled water
☐ Connection cards

and cracker snacks. Or you could provide a wrapped pastry and coffee in cold weather. In the summer, switch to sealed cold drinks such as bottled water or individual-serving juice cans.

How do you find people who need a bus token?
Get a map of the bus stops from the local public transportation entity, and hit popular bus stops in urban areas.

40 BUS RUNS

This creative project sounds more complicated than it is, so keep an open mind. It doesn't take a lot of people to pull this off. We did it with just a few people when we first planted our church in Cincinnati.

WHAT YOU'LL NEED

- □ A good used school bus
- □ Clothes and food racks
- □ Sized and separated clothes
- □ Connection cards

First, purchase a used school bus. If you haven't checked into the market, you'll find them surprisingly affordable—under three thousand dollars. Bring a skilled mechanic to be sure you're getting a dependable bus. Take out some or all of the seats and install clothes racks and shelves for bags of food. Outfitting the bus is a great project for those skilled in design and carpentry. Add steps for the rear exit, including handrails. Make sure it's narrow enough to fit through the back door for storage when the bus is in transit.

If you can, license the bus as a truck because, in many states, insurance and driving stipulations will be significantly relaxed. Be sure to check the laws in your own state.

How do you find people who could benefit from a bus run?
Drive and park at a low-income housing area. Invite people by knocking on doors and saying, "We're here to show you God's kindness in a practical way. We have free food and clothes for those in need. If you or anyone you know needs any, send them over!"

Assign teams of two to walk people home. These teams can help people carry what they've chosen from the bus, as well as talk, listen, and pray for them.

41 RONALD MCDONALD HOUSE OUTREACH DELUXE

WHAT YOU'LL NEED

- □ Food
- □ Nice table settings
- □ Gift baskets
- □ Connection cards

Ronald McDonald Houses are homes that were established for out-of-town families of children staying at nearby hospitals. Many churches do outreach by providing meals for families staying at these homes. This outreach is always well received and appreciated.

Take it a step further. Use a linen

tablecloth, cloth napkins, fine china, silverware, a centerpiece, flowers, and seasonal decorations. Provide a fancy dinner with live music.

Many families are stuck in waiting at this point in their lives. So, in addition to people who bring food, service, and special music, be sure your team includes listeners who can talk with and pray for these families.

Consider leaving each family a basket of goodies; include Post-It notes, pens, gum, hand lotion, candy, and an inspirational book.

How do you find people who could use a special outreach at a Ronald McDonald House?
Check with hospital chaplains or with the director of the Ronald McDonald House to see which families are particularly in need of cheering-up visits.

42 CHEMO-LOUNGE SINGERS

Many people on chemotherapy actively deal with depression. They aren't sure what the future holds. Children receiving treatment are confused. And their families struggle to hold on to hope.

The best way to deal with enormously stressful spiritual and emotional struggles isn't to try harder to fight the battle, but to build hope.

Sing fun songs that aren't too churchy—ones people know and can join in on. These songs can bring hope even if they aren't overtly Christian. The Christian songs you sing also need to be upbeat, big on hope and a positive future. Often you'll see doctors and nurses listening in as well.

WHAT YOU'LL NEED

- ☐ People who can lead songs
- ☐ Pray-ers
- ☐ Talented listeners

How do you find people who would be encouraged by the Chemo-Lounge Singers?
Contact hospital chaplains to see who is in need of encouragement. Also, once word of your unusual ministry leaks out, people will contact you to come in and encourage their relatives.

43 GROCERY RUNS WITH "GOD MONEY"

This is a great project that has a one-two punch—it helps the needy and it helps children to learn the joy of giving. Set aside part of the offerings, or "God money," from children's Sunday school classes or children's church to go to a special fund for the needy. Collect money until it accrues to a point that they can buy several bags of food. Parents then match the money with an offering of their own. The children pick out the food at the grocery store (with some low-key assistance from their parents).

WHAT YOU'LL NEED

□ Some willing children
□ Groceries

After purchasing the food, parents and children drive around and ask God to show them where to give the groceries away. Children learn a bit about how to listen for God's voice and guidance. They also experience the joy of giving beyond themselves to strangers. It is particularly powerful for them to be able to see where their purchases are going, to personally participate in the giving away of these goodies.

How do you find people who would be helped by a grocery run? Go with the prayer-driving approach. Otherwise you can ask around in a needy neighborhood for those who have a need for groceries.

44 WELCOME WAGON FOR IMMIGRANTS AND REFUGEES

If you've ever lived in or even visited a foreign country, you know how incredibly isolating it can be to not understand much of the local ways, including where to shop. You can build bridges to newcomers to this country by taking them shopping and orienting them to their new city.

WHAT YOU'LL NEED

□ Good maps of your city
□ Transportation
□ Language translators
□ Connection cards

The concept behind this project isn't to buy goods, but to be a tour guide for new residents who don't know much about their new city or country.

How do you find immigrants and refugees in need of a welcome wagon?

People of common nationality tend to live together in apartment complexes. Once you run into one or two families who are new to the country, you'll often find many more families to reach.

45 BABY GIFT BAGS FOR NEW MOTHERS

Many needy people have babies who are never celebrated—no baby shower! You can help a little by filling a bright baby bag with items such as diapers, a bib, a small blanket, a Christian children's Bible or story book, a rattle, a pacifier, baby powder, baby wipes, an inspirational book for Mom, a Scripture tape on prayer (see project 23), and so on.

WHAT YOU'LL NEED

□ Baby gift bags
□ Goodies for the bags
□ Connection cards

If your church has a young married group, you might encourage them to take ownership of this project.

This bridge helps you meet people who are having babies—particularly teens and twentysomething single mothers. Let them know the other things you're providing through your ministries to the community.

How do you find people who need baby bags?

If you've begun to minister regularly in a needy neighborhood or housing complex, you can easily find out when babies are born. Or connect with local hospital chaplains and with those who are already involved in your ministries to the needy.

46 INSPIRATIONAL CALENDARS

Homeless people living on the streets easily lose track of dates. Others in need also appreciate a good calendar. Instead of a generic calendar, consider creating custom-made calendars with inspiring photos. Include holiday and local events that needy people would find helpful and want to be involved in throughout the year. You can also

WHAT YOU'LL NEED

□ Calendar-making computer software
□ Digital photos
□ Inspirational sayings
□ Access to a self-serve copy center

highlight services that needy people might not be aware of.

You can easily create calendars with your own digital photos and a computer. Most printer software includes calendar programs. But if those don't fit your needs, you can purchase a program for as little as thirty dollars. Putting this together, once you find good photos, isn't too difficult. Check out www.stevesjogren.com for several hundred thought-provoking inspirational sayings.

How do you find people in need of an inspirational calendar?
Look for homeless people and ask other needy people you're already connecting with.

47 PARK WORSHIP

Nothing breaks down walls and barriers between people easier than live music. Set up your band in a park. Include fun, sing-along songs as well as worship choruses. If you draw a more senior-oriented crowd, don't be afraid to perform some hymns and patriotic songs. Wherever you perform, choose songs that are easy to join in with—ones most people would know.

WHAT YOU'LL NEED

- ☐ Decent musicians
- ☐ Instruments
- ☐ Song sheets
- ☐ Connection cards

A nice touch is to bring along instruments for the neighborhood to play, especially rhythm instruments like tambourines, bongos, congas, and maracas.

How do you find people who would appreciate worship in the park?
If you start to play and have some good quality to what you do, you'll easily attract a crowd.

48 FIXING UP DWELLINGS

Few things communicate that you value people as much as helping them with their dwellings. It doesn't take highly trained professionals to make a visible and sometimes remarkable difference in a family's housing. A team of just a half-dozen eager volunteers armed with screwdrivers and paintbrushes can make short work of an elderly person's apartment or a single mom's home in need of attention.

Some of the most common projects to get involved with include:

- Painting front doors
- Replacing plastic light switches and outlet covers
- Replacing light bulbs
- Moving things they can't

This is a particularly great project for the senior adults in your congregation.

How do you find people who would appreciate having their dwelling fixed up?
Knock on doors and say, "Hi, we're doing some small fix-up projects for people in the neighborhood to show God's love in a practical way. Do you need any help with a project or do you know any neighbors who need some help?"

WHAT YOU'LL NEED

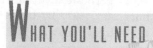

- ☐ Screwdrivers
- ☐ Cans of paint (neutral or complementary colors)
- ☐ Paintbrushes
- ☐ Sandpaper
- ☐ Paintbrush cleaner
- ☐ Plastic light switch and outlet covers
- ☐ Light bulbs
- ☐ Stepladders
- ☐ Connection cards

49 ROBIN HOOD OUTREACH—WHEELBARROW FOOD COLLECTION

Okay, maybe this project is slightly misnamed. You're not actually stealing from the rich, but you are receiving from those who "have" and giving to those who "don't have." Go door to door in suburban neighborhoods to ask for food to give to people who are needy. Roll a wheelbarrow up the driveway, knock on the door, and ask if they would like to give food items that will be given to single-parent families. You'll rarely be turned down! Deep down, most people want to do something to help others who are less fortunate than they are. Be sure to thank them!

WHAT YOU'LL NEED

- ☐ Wheelbarrow
- ☐ Smiles
- ☐ Connection cards

How do you find people to receive food from?
Wheel around suburban neighborhoods.

50 BACK-TO-SCHOOL PARTY

Going back to school in the fall is reason to celebrate, but education is not equally celebrated in all families. You can create a festive atmosphere around the joy of going back to school.

Part of the party is giving gifts—school supplies, lunch snacks, new socks. Be creative. Play games with the children, serve food, and invite the parents to participate. At the end of the party, pray for the children to have a successful year in school and to enjoy themselves.

WHAT YOU'LL NEED

- ☐ Party supplies
- ☐ Gifts
- ☐ Connection cards

This is an appropriate project for a Sunday school class to take ownership of. Try to identify a community liaison to help you connect what your church has to offer with those in the area you are helping.

How do you find people who would enjoy a back-to-school party?
Contact local school principals—to help identify needy families or neighborhoods—as well as those you've already gotten to know through other ministries to the needy.

51 BIG PARTIES

Who doesn't like a good party? There's just something electric about parties that makes them larger than life. Capitalize on the buzz of a party by throwing one to bring the kingdom of God closer by action, word, and deed. Some of the parties you can sponsor include:

Candlelight Dinners in the Park
Set up a nice dinner in the park with tablecloths. Go over the top. Use plastic champagne glasses with 7-Up. Serve the nicest food you can muster. Candles will make this one close to fine dining in the park.

Matthew's Parties
Matthew, the apostle and former tax collector, threw a big party to celebrate when he first was introduced to Jesus. He invited all his friends who hadn't yet met Jesus. Matthew's Parties have the same

flavor—to celebrate meeting Jesus! Have a cookout combined with a lot of games, prizes, and a major atmosphere-building event. Be sure that everything is free. Invade an inner-city park for a few hours with free food, drinks, games, music, and door prizes. Bring along plenty of trash bags for clean up afterward.

A video of a Matthew's Party in action can be purchased online at www.kindness.com or by calling toll free at 1-888-KINDNESS.

Lamb's Lunches
Hold an outdoor sit-down dinner for the homeless. Serve something easy and filling such as spaghetti and meatballs. Over the years, our church has become famous for having Cincinnati's largest meatballs—that's something good to be famous for among the street population! This one is intended to be a conversational time between the servers and the served, so be sure to have a lot of volunteers staffing the event.

"BBQ (The Name of Your Town Here)"
This is a blow-out barbecue for the needy done on a grand scale. Include plenty of games, giveaways, and even pony rides. (Every kid needs to have a pony ride in his or her childhood.) This is one impressive party!

Other elements you can include at this party:
• A cake walk
• Bike repairs
• Invite the local police and fire departments to join in the event with bike and scooter registrations. Kids love checking out the fire trucks.
• A clown

WHAT YOU'LL NEED

☐ Prizes
☐ Puppets and skits
☐ Bubbles
☐ Contests

And you can give away the following:
• Refurbished computers
• TVs and VCRs
• Restaurant gift certificates
• Christian bookstore gift certificates
• Christian CDs
• Items donated by local Christian businesses
• Helium balloons
• Balloon animals

How do you find people to come to big parties?
Set up in a park and distribute flyers. Also, word of mouth carries quickly.

52 INFLATABLE PILLOWS FOR THE HOMELESS

Homeless people can always use some comfort as they fend for themselves on the streets. When sleeping on a park bench or on the ground or in a homeless shelter, it's great to have one's own pil-low. Because it's inflatable, this kind of pillow can be deflated to take up less room and will be lighter to carry around. You can probably find this personal item for about five dollars each.

WHAT YOU'LL NEED

☐ Inflatable pillows
☐ Connection cards

How do you find people who could use inflatable pillows?
Approach homeless people in parks and ask homeless shelter directors if you can distribute pillows at the centers.

53 SHOE SHINING—MODERN-DAY FOOT WASHING

These days most people don't need a literal foot washing as much as they might need their shoes cleaned and shined. Homeless people are in their shoes close to 24/7, so their shoes are usually in need of a good cleaning every few days. This is a great project because anyone who lives on the streets can really use it, and any volunteer with a little bit of patience can learn to give a good shoe polish. It's been said there's nothing like a haircut and shoe shine to adjust one's outlook on life! This project will prove half of that statement!

WHAT YOU'LL NEED

☐ Shoe polish
☐ Shoe treatment
☐ Suede brush
☐ Shoelaces
☐ Shoe polishing brushes
☐ Connection cards

How do you find people to give a shine to?
Everywhere! Just look for the slightly messy shoes.

54 TWO GUYS AND A TRUCK—WITH A TWIST

Moving is always a hassle among needy people—whether they're dealing with issues of immobility due to disabilities, or they lack transportation, or they're elderly. You remove the hassle by making the move free and easy.

While "Two Guys and a Truck" is the name of a popular moving company, you'll be better off with about six guys on this project! That way, everyone involved will have a lot more fun.

How do you find people to move?
Offer your services by distributing flyers in needy areas. You will have no shortage of takers!

WHAT YOU'LL NEED

- ☐ Strong guys with good backs
- ☐ Moving dollies
- ☐ Moving blankets
- ☐ Pickup trucks
- ☐ Connection cards

LEVEL 2

RECONCILIATION—SEEING PEOPLE GET RIGHT WITH GOD AND ONE ANOTHER

OKAY, YOU'VE TAKEN THE first baby steps in ministry to people in need. You've met some needs! But now it's time to take the next step. The projects in this section focus on right relationships. This is ministry that offers opportunity to lead others to Christ.

When people get right with God, they often realize their need to get right with one another as well. It's difficult to truly be reconciled with God and not try to reconcile with our fellow human beings pretty quickly.

HOW TO LEAD SOMEONE TO CHRIST

Many people are intimidated by the idea of actually praying with someone to receive Christ. Perhaps your faith tradition doesn't emphasize the concept of "receiving Christ." Language aside, many adults haven't clarified their relationship with God. They might have a childlike faith in God, but they don't have a specific relationship with Jesus Christ as their Savior. Clarifying this relationship is a powerful, life-changing, transforming experience.

Oddly, most "evangelical" Christians have never successfully led anyone to Christ. In fact, most have never even attempted to share their faith with an unchurched person.

Why? Some people think it's a lack of training in the church, but we don't buy that. While we could always use more and better training, we don't see the problem as simply a lack of training. In my more than twenty years as a leader in the church, we've never seen *any* problem that boiled down to a lack of training.

We're sure that our lack of evangelism effectiveness is complex. But toward the top of the list of reasons is motivation. We simply don't do evangelism because very few of us think we *can* do evangelism. It's seen as something that highly spiritual people do.

How would things be different in the church if we all saw evangelism as something so simple that anyone could do it effectively?

Keep it loving.
Don't be pushy.

Keep it real.
For example, say things like, "Christ has begun to change my life."

Keep it straight.
God is for you. He isn't angry with you. He understands you completely. There's no reason to run from him. He's seen all that you've done; yet he approaches you and invites you to have a relationship with him. He's making that invitation through me right here and now. He's made that invitation in Scripture through his Son (John 3:16).

God forgives me and you. All I know about the forgiveness of God is what I've learned from knowing his forgiveness personally. I've seen what he can do by forgiving a person from the inside out. It is a cleansing work that is the most powerful thing a person can experience in life.

God can change a life—mine and yours. He has changed me. Even me! He can change you as well. I know from experience.

Keep it simple.
I'm all for training. Many programs are circulating in the church to help Christians share their faith. Be able "to give an answer for the hope that is in you." Practice telling the high points of your own journey of faith in Christ.

Keep the prayer simple.
Well God, here I am. When the people in Scripture came face to face with God, they often responded to that setting with the words, "Here I am." The prayer of availability is the most profoundly simple yet basic prayer that exists. It covers the gamut of human desires toward God. Nothing is deeper or more comprehensive. I have prayed this prayer with hundreds of people and seen it connect with them at a deeply spiritual level.

Keep people connected.
Help people find a Christian friend who can help and encourage them. Look for someone somewhat within their natural circle of influence, not an official "discipler appointee."

55 FOOD PANTRY

A food pantry is one of the most universal outreaches to the needy. When we first began a ministry to the needy, we immediately received calls for food. So we started our first tiny pantry.

Decide how long your food pantry will be open. Be real—it's going to be difficult to man your operation more than three days a week for half a day at a time.

As government programs shrink and disappear, people are more in need of food assistance than ever. Here are a few different approaches to doing a food pantry:

Simple Is Better
Simply supply bags of groceries, prayer, and a lot of smiles. Not high on atmosphere, but plenty of food to go around. This has few moving components, just meeting needs in the community directly and effectively.

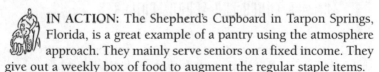

WHAT YOU'LL NEED

☐ Shelving
☐ Atmosphere music
☐ Connection cards

Going for Atmosphere
This is just the opposite idea. Provide an inviting place to talk, serve coffee, and have some great atmosphere music going, coffeehouse style. Cheerfully help people carry groceries out to cars.

IN ACTION: The Shepherd's Cupboard in Tarpon Springs, Florida, is a great example of a pantry using the atmosphere approach. They mainly serve seniors on a fixed income. They give out a weekly box of food to augment the regular staple items.

Full-Tilt Boogie
Shoot the works! This is the full treatment. Treat people like you would want to be treated—and then some.

IN ACTION: Vineyard Christian Fellowship in Hamilton, Ohio, has an all-out pantry complete with soft background music and a living-room setting. Pantry users are offered donuts or bagels and a cappuccino by someone wearing a colorful apron. While waiting to be served, people are escorted to a reading area stocked with the latest magazines and best-sellers. It's enough to brighten any spirit!

How do you find people in need of a pantry?
Connect with state caseworkers to see who is in need of additional food to see them through the month. Once you get started, word of mouth will quickly spread that you have food available.

56 FOOD AND MINISTRY CO-OP

This project is slightly different from a pantry; it offers "a hand up instead of a handout."

In a cooperative, all who receive help also give help. The rule to those who receive help is, "The first installment of food is free, but after that you need to work to help others."

A community is built by those who are both givers and receivers. Other projects are cooperatively done together to help those in need. Many of our most creative projects aimed at the needy have been manned by the members of our cooperative.

WHAT YOU'LL NEED

☐ Facility
☐ Source for food
☐ Energetic volunteers
☐ Strong leadership

How do you find people in need of a ministry co-op?
Look for the same sorts of people who are interested in being part of a pantry.

57 SUMMER LUNCH FOR SCHOOL CHILDREN

Children from needy families often receive proper nutrition each day based on the lunch provided by the school. But when school lets out for the summer, so does that predictable midday meal.

WHAT YOU'LL NEED

☐ Food
☐ Facility
☐ Friendly, high-energy volunteers
☐ Connection cards

Losing this meal is more than just the loss of lunch—it often is the loss of the main meal of the day for children in need. This lack of balanced nutrition causes several problems, including a propensity toward fighting, mischief, scuffles with the law, and a lack of motivation to return to school in the fall.

How do you find children who need a summer lunch?
Look for children in public places like parks or low-income apartment complexes. Once you establish a relationship with them, you'll have steady traffic for the rest of the summer.

58 THE MAGDALENE PROJECT

One class of needy people rarely reached by the church is women trapped in prostitution and the sex industry (like stripping). This project is a dignified way of connecting with women who are caught in these lifestyles.

It originated with a woman who was a former waitress in a strip club. She saw up close the cycle of entrapment that kept women enslaved in this lifestyle. She began to reach out to them, at first at Easter with baskets that expressed love and compassion. Complete with the contents listed here and a touching note, the baskets were received with tears of gratitude. Most appreciated were the stuffed animals—a lot of women in this industry began at surprisingly young ages and had their childhoods stolen. These stuffed animals are an attempt to return a little bit of innocence to them.

Since its inception, The Magdalene Project has expanded beyond Easter to include regular weekend distribution in a number of cities including Atlanta, Austin, Las Vegas, Reno, Dallas, Phoenix, and Kingston, New York.

Check out the website at www.themagdaleneproject.org. (Make sure you spell "Magdalene" correctly.)

The following is the text of the "Mary note" to be placed in each bag.

WHAT YOU'LL NEED

Street basket:
☐ Basket or gift bag
☐ Makeup
☐ Lotions
☐ Shampoo
☐ Sunscreen
☐ "Mary note"

Club basket:
☐ Basket or gift bag
☐ Fingernail polish
☐ Inspirational gift
☐ Cross
☐ Flashlight with "Jesus is the light" on it
☐ Inspirational pencil and pad
☐ Breath mints
☐ Candy
☐ Bubbles
☐ Stuffed animal
☐ "Mary note"

Did you know there is a very important person in the Bible named Mary Magdalene? You may have heard of her. There are strong indications that she was a "Lady of the Evening" and most certainly, a woman of "reputation."

It's probably safe to say that Mary Magdalene had experienced a lot of rejection, abuse, and abandonment in her young life. She probably knew what it was to feel pain every day, and she longed for a different life. She was tormented by her own personal demons and controlled by her circumstances.

Then one day, she met Jesus and began to listen to his teachings. He may have been the first man who gave to her instead of taking from her. He silenced the tormenting demons and gave her a new life of value, purpose, and respect.

Just when things were getting better for her, Jesus was arrested and brutally beaten! Mary Magdalene was devastated. Her once-hardened heart was broken as she watched in horror when Jesus was nailed to a cross. She must have felt like she had lost everything that was good in her life. He had done so many other miracles. Why did he allow this to happen? She didn't realize he chose to hang there paying the price for her sins—and ours. Yes, despite her past, he really loved her that much.

Three days later, still reeling with grief, Mary Magdalene made her way to the tomb to anoint Jesus' body with burial spices and fragrant oils. But all she found was an empty tomb. She was more confused than ever. Someone must have taken the body away.

Through her tear-swollen eyes, she saw a figure and thought it must be the gardener. He asked her, "Why are you crying? Who are you looking for?" She responded, "Sir, if you've taken him away, tell me where you have laid him, and I will get him." What determination she displayed.

Instead of answering her question, Jesus spoke one word to her. He spoke her name—"Mary." With that word, he acknowledged her personhood, her dignity, her identity. Jesus knew and recognized her even before she recognized him. When he called her by name, her grief vanished. She turned her focus from death to victory. She realized he had been in charge all along, even in her darkest hour. Suddenly her eyes were open and she saw him in all his loving splendor. Because of his love and his resurrection, her life was changed forever.

The first Easter began that Sunday morning as God's power came like a thunderbolt, giving Jesus victory over death, hell, and the grave. Jesus was resurrected from the dead! All the angels in heaven began celebrating, rejoicing, and praising God.

But on earth, the celebration couldn't begin until Jesus appeared to someone. Jesus didn't choose his disciples or his mother or anyone else. He chose Mary Magdalene!

Many well-meaning people across the world will celebrate Easter in beautiful churches with nice clothes and great music. That's great . . . but it's not how Jesus chose to celebrate Easter. He first gave the Easter message to Mary Magdalene, a person disapproved of by the world, a person who had experienced many hurtful things from those who should have loved her.

Many of us feel like Mary Magdalene. Perhaps you identify with her, too.

As God has shown us how Jesus celebrated the first Easter, we feel very sad because so many people have celebrated Easter without Mary Magdalene. We are so very sorry that the very people that Jesus loved so much have been left out of traditional Easter celebrations. We ask you to please accept our apology and forgive our ignorance.

If you're living a life that reflects your inner pain, Jesus wants to reveal his love and acceptance to you . . . even as he did to Mary Magdalene almost two thousand years ago.

May this (Easter) gift be a blessing to you. It represents God's grace and open heart for you. We all need that. There's a little bit of Mary Magdalene in all of us. Our prayer is that you will come to know Jesus just like Mary Magdalene did that first Easter morning. Your life will never be the same either. He truly loves you, and he calls your name. If you would like to talk more about this message please call: _____.

How do you find people in need of The Magdalene Project?
Ask police where the street people are, and ask street preachers in urban areas where the prostitutes live and work. You can also go directly to strip clubs, especially if you can take someone along who is an ex-stripper. Finally, you can also visit women's prisons through chaplains, and you can give any woman in jail one of these bags.

59 BIG CHRISTMAS PARTY

People in need don't always celebrate Christmas properly because there aren't Christ-centered celebration opportunities. You can sponsor an event that will be fun and will cause everyone to focus on Jesus.

The elements of this celebration include playing games and singing songs. As you sing Christmas carols, make sure the words are available. It's also fun to have a few inexpensive rhythm instruments available for people to play along with.

Someone can share what Christmas is about in a very positive and upbeat way—simply explaining, "Christmas is important to me because . . ."

Decorations and refreshments or a meal can be simple or elaborate depending on the inclination of the group.

For about one dollar per photo you can take Polaroid pictures of kids with an ethnically correct Santa. Design a simple backdrop and get up close with the camera. Mount the photo on red or green construction paper and add the child's name and the year in a gold or silver marking pen.

At the conclusion of the party, give away small gifts as people depart—perhaps a Bible or a devotional book. Consider giving away the decorations as well.

WHAT YOU'LL NEED

- ☐ Facility
- ☐ Polaroid camera
- ☐ Film
- ☐ Construction paper
- ☐ Glue sticks
- ☐ Gold and silver marking pens
- ☐ Refreshments
- ☐ Connection cards

How do you find people who would enjoy a Christmas party?
Invite those who are already connected with your ministry to the needy. Give out flyers or invitations at previous events in the neighborhood. Or simply walk the neighborhoods and distribute flyers.

60 KID'S CLUB

Children between five and ten have a great interest in being part of a "club." Unfortunately, that's why gangs are popular in many needy neighborhoods. Start a club that is redemptive for kids in need. A weekly club held in a needy neighborhood is a great way to make an investment into children's lives and in their families as well.

Do the outreach once a week for ninety minutes from approximately 6:30 to 8:00 P.M.

Do a brief Bible study and cement the lesson with a related activity or craft. Encourage kids to share the activity and Bible story with their parents. And encourage them to memorize short Scripture verses.

Relationships form best when the kids have regular teachers. The idea is to play games, have fun, learn something, and for the kids to feel loved! Pass out a lot of hugs.

It's great for men to help out. So many of the children who'll come don't have a healthy male role model.

WHAT YOU'LL NEED

☐ Craft supplies
☐ Facility
☐ Refreshments
☐ Connection cards

How do you find kids in need of a kid's club?
Contact the principal of the school located in the neighborhood you're working in to see if he or she will let you advertise. You can also connect with children who are already coming to other activities you're sponsoring for the needy. When you're deciding on a location for your club, be sure to take into account the traveling distances for the children and other limitations they may face.

61 DOOR-TO-DOOR HEALTH CARE WITH DOCTORS, NURSES, AND MEDICINE

A doctor friend who was just starting a practice in our area closed his office one day a week. Together we'd go out to care for street people with medical needs. We did a variety of medical procedures, but found that some health problems were more common than others. (By the way, this doctor's new practice was amazingly blessed by God. In spite of closing one day a week to care for the needy, his practice grew.)

Find a doctor or a group of physicians willing to do a similar

WHAT YOU'LL NEED

- Medications
- Basic medical equipment: blood pressure cup, ear scope, flashlight, thermometer with plastic covers, stethoscope
- Connection cards

outreach. You'll figure out quickly what the most common ailments are in your area. Stock up on supplies and medications needed for those ailments. Many pharmaceutical companies will donate sample medications to stock you.

Most of the needy who need medical care—including many senior citizens and prostitutes—have ample access to medical help if they'd simply go out and find it. But many of these people are not motivated to seek such help due to fear, low self-esteem, or lack of understanding of the value of it. Some see going to a doctor or a clinic as a last resort and simply won't go to a doctor until they are very ill.

How do you find people in need of in-home health care?
Approach people door to door or in public places like parks. Say, "Hi, we're a team of doctors and nurses who are Christians showing God's love in a practical way. Do you know of anyone who needs health care in the neighborhood?" By asking in this way, you give them the freedom to tell you they personally have a need for help, or they can direct you to someone down the block.

62 CAMPS FOR KIDS

Anyone who went to camp as a child remembers the power of a camp to transform the heart in a matter of a few hours or days. You can hold a camp for children in need. These are like a Vacation Bible School in a needy neighborhood.

WHAT YOU'LL NEED

- Camp supplies
- Facilities
- T-shirts
- Godly role models
- Certificates and trophies for campers
- Silly awards for the leaders

Bring in a speaker who will relate the similarities between the camp topic and walking with God. Make sure you find someone kids will relate to, not someone stuffy and unfriendly.

Sports Camp—A One-Day Event
Consider making it two hours for junior-high and three hours for high-

school students later in the day. Award trophies for athletic contests and sports quizzes. Advertise in local schools via flyers.

Hero Day Camp
Work on different sports each day. Invite a local professional athlete or a prominent college athlete each day. The thrust of this camp is to introduce local sports heroes, but also to introduce Jesus as the ultimate hero.

Mini-Bike Camp
This can be sponsored by a local motorcycle dealer. Kids get to ride mini-bikes with permission of their parents and the sponsors, who help teach safety, maintenance, care, and respect for bikes. Kids earn the right to go to the mini-bike camp by turning in all their school homework for the week—making it a privilege to be a part of this camp.

Skaters' Camp
Recruit a local teen skater to teach kids moves. Build ramps, get insurance waivers, and make sure parents sign a safety agreement and an emergency medical release before skaters come onto the property.

How do you find kids who would benefit from a camp?
Ask school counselors.

IN ACTION: Church in the City in Denver started with the intent of reaching the needy in creative ways. Since their start-up in the late 1980s, they've met in a number of creative facilities that have led up to their current location—a former Safeway store in a troubled part of the city. The church has dozens of outreach projects that have attracted an activist following of more than one thousand people of every socioeconomic strata from around the city. Some people walk to church, others take public transportation, while a few drive late-model Porsches. But all have hearts for the needy.

63 BUS MINISTRY TRANSPORTING FAMILIES TO VISIT PRISONS

Drive family members of prisoners to prison facilities that are within two or three hours of your area once per month. Take turns going to different prisons on different Saturdays. (See project 40 for information on purchasing a bus.)

WHAT YOU'LL NEED

- ☐ Worship team
- ☐ Bus
- ☐ Insurance-approved drivers

Meet at a central location convenient for the families. Have a time of worship before getting on the bus. Pray for the day. Ask for God's blessing before leaving the parking lot.

How do you find people in need of transportation to prisons?
Jail or prison chaplains will know who is in need.

 IN ACTION: Church in the City in Denver has done this for some years. They now take ninety people per week in fifteen-passenger vans. Those doing this ministry are developing relationships with the families on the way to and from the prisons—as well as afterward.

64 HEALTH CLINIC

You set up a clinic that's essentially a doctor's office, but the services offered are completely free. Because it is staffed by doctors, you will be able to prescribe medications; sample medications provided by pharmaceutical companies can be offered for free as well.

WHAT YOU'LL NEED

- ☐ Facility with at least one private examination room
- ☐ Capacity to schedule appointments
- ☐ Doctor
- ☐ Nurses
- ☐ Donated medications
- ☐ Connection cards

Here are some common services you can offer:

- Physical examinations
- Health screenings
- Sick patient care

Be sure to limit office hours to what you and the volunteer physicians can handle. You can apply for grant money, but the granting agency could dictate what hours you must stay open, the number of patients you need to see, and the sorts of patients you need to focus on.

How do you find people in need of a health clinic?
In addition to serving people already involved with your other ministries to the needy, do some public relations work. Make your services known through newspaper interviews. When word gets

out about what you're doing, you will probably gain some decent media coverage, and people will come to your clinic.

 IN ACTION: Check out the health clinic of Heartland Community Church, Lawrence, Kansas, at their church's website (www.hcclawrence.com).

65 PERSONAL DEVELOPMENT—ANGER MANAGEMENT/CONFLICT RESOLUTION

Many people don't get decent employment opportunities because they lack personal and social skills. Tremendous support can be found in small groups, but the needy are often isolated from good support systems.

Offer classes that are designed to help make up for lost time. A couple of books to consider studying are *The Dance of Anger* by Harriet Lerner (HarperCollins, 1997) and *The Anger Workbook* by Carter, Minrith, and Meier (Thomas Nelson, 1993).

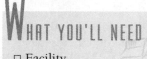 **WHAT YOU'LL NEED**
□ Facility
□ Teachers
□ Books

Be sure to offer classes that are in a safe public place, such as a church or community center, not in a home. Find skilled presenters and apprentice assistants.

Set ground rules:

- No counseling or advice giving.
- Attendees use "I" messages when sharing.
- Seek to get everyone to share during the meeting.
- Encourage dominating people to talk after the group instead of during the group.
- Encourage the sharing of praise reports at the beginning of the meeting.
- Reserve prayer requests for the end of the meeting.

How do you find people in need of—and open to—personal development classes?
Connect with local police and with other ministries that are caring for the needy, such as the Salvation Army.

66 PERSONAL DEVELOPMENT—ADDICTION ISSUES

For this project, you'll essentially be starting a twelve-step group for people dealing with addiction issues. Many needy people need to deal with habits that have kept them in bondage before they can make any other forward progress. Without freedom from their addictions, all the other help in the world isn't going to add up to much.

A great text for launching out is *Search for Significance* by Robert S. McGee (Word, 1998).

WHAT YOU'LL NEED

□ Coffee
□ Meeting room
□ Storage for snacks and supplies

How do you find people in need of—and open to—dealing with addiction issues?
Call the Alcoholics Anonymous central offices of your city or district to offer your church's location for meetings in your area.

67 NURSING HOME PET PARADE

Nursing home residents often live a boring and lonely existence. You can bring a little life to their lives by bringing in an animal parade.

Bring a variety of animals, from puppies and kittens to potbelly pigs and tropical fish. For additional fun, have children dress up their pets for the pet parade. Be sure the pets are gentle around strange people. Keep the pets on leashes and under the control of the owners.

WHAT YOU'LL NEED

□ Interesting animals
□ People good with the care of animals
□ Volunteers who are gentle and patient with the elderly
□ Connection cards

How do you find a nursing home in which to do a pet parade?
Contact several nursing homes with your idea. Take your mini-zoo on the road for several stops on a given day. Do that once a month until you've reached a dozen or more nursing homes. After several months, return to the original nursing home and start over.

68 NURSING HOME SPECIAL DAY REMEMBRANCES

Special days often go uncelebrated in the lives of seniors. The life of a person in a nursing home is mostly composed of memories of many decades of a well-spent life. Many of these people enjoy just talking to someone about what they've lived through. This gives them a chance to reflect on and celebrate the great things that they've survived and accomplished through the years.

With a little help from their friends (that's you), special days on the calendar can be reinforced as special. These days include Christmas, birthdays, Mother's Day, Independence Day, Valentine's Day, and Memorial Day. Use some of these ideas to bring some love and hugs to older folks in need of emotional encouragement.

Personalize small stockings or ornaments at Christmas-time and sing a few carols while you're there. Give flowers or a small gift on Valentine's Day or Sweetest Day. On the Fourth of July, distribute small American flags and sing patriotic songs. On Father's or Mother's Day, come in with a Polaroid and take the residents' photos.

WHAT YOU'LL NEED

☐ Greeting cards
☐ Candies
☐ Flowers
☐ Polaroid camera
☐ Warm and patient volunteers
☐ Connection cards

How do you find nursing home patients who are in need?
Call nursing home managers or activity directors to explain your projects. See if they're open to what you want to do.

69 MENTORING PAROLEES

The whole idea of prison in our culture is that upon their release from prison, parolees have been rehabilitated to live in society again. It's one thing to have gone through an official program, perhaps to have graduated from a halfway house, but quite another to transition to a place of strength, hope, and healing in life.

WHAT YOU'LL NEED

☐ A place to meet
☐ A book to study together

You can become a mentor to new parolees. This mostly involves spending quality time in a consistent way with these impressionable people. A good way to organize these meetings is to study a book together. A great book that serves as a good conversation starter is *Love, Acceptance and Forgiveness* by Jerry Cook (Gospel Light, 1979).

How do you find parolees in need of mentoring?
Ask prison chaplains. Of course, it's best for men to mentor male parolees, women to mentor female parolees.

70 SHOES FOR KIDS GOING BACK TO SCHOOL

Children returning to school need some encouragement to take pride in their work. A new pair of shoes is a simple but effective tool for boosting the morale of children.

This is a project that volunteers in your church will be eager to participate in. Encourage families to buy a second pair of shoes the same size as their own child's when they go shoe shopping.

WHAT YOU'LL NEED

□ Shoes from an inexpensive source
□ Connection cards

How do you find kids in need of shoes?
Look for children who live in low-income housing areas. Ask school officials.

71 FIRST-AID KITS

Many needy people simply don't have a first-aid kit. You might focus on assembling and distributing kits for people with children.

You don't have to spend a lot on packaging—you can even put the items in a large Ziplock bag and put a red cross sticker on the bag. Instead of a connection card, you can place a label on the bag with the same information to advertise your

WHAT YOU'LL NEED

□ Non-aspirin pain reliever
□ Bandages of different sizes
□ Scissors
□ Tweezers
□ Gauze
□ Q-Tips
□ Latex gloves
□ Tape
□ Triple antibiotic ointment
□ Anti-itch cream
□ Chapstick
□ Ipecac syrup
□ Sunscreen
□ Connection cards

church as a long-term contact for the future.

Be sure to indicate if people can call to restock the items in the bags.

How do you find people in need of first-aid kits?
Connect with people who are already receiving care from other ministries you have going.

72 SHELTER CENTER MINISTRY

People who frequent shelters have a place of refuge during harsh weather. But there are drawbacks to finding care at shelters. Typically, people aren't allowed to shower unless they have clean underwear to change into. Also, toiletries are at a premium and usually aren't supplied by the centers. And there's always a need for great listeners. Your team can provide for all of these needs.

If you've never done any ministry to shelter center residents, you'll be surprised at the amazing cross section of people who find their way to these places. You can't judge a book by its cover!

How do you help people in shelters?
Contact the directors of local shelters.

WHAT YOU'LL NEED
□ Toiletries
□ New underwear
□ Socks
□ Caring listeners
□ Connection cards

73 DROP INN BUS

Think of a bus that is outfitted like a family room, one that creates a comfortable atmosphere for talking and simply "hanging out" with street people. (See project 40 for comments on purchasing a bus.) Design the bus with tables and soft lights throughout. Add a couple of shelves to store goods for those you will be serving.

Park right in front of ministry centers and shelter centers. Invite residents to "hang out," drink coffee, and

WHAT YOU'LL NEED
□ Bus
□ Cookies
□ Coffee
□ Cream
□ Sugar
□ Sweetener
□ Cups
□ Stir sticks
□ Napkins
□ Connection cards

just talk with people from your church. You can also offer toiletries, a new pair of underwear, socks, and in the winter, a coat if they need one. Gloves, scarves, shirts, and pants are also popular giveaway items.

Ministering to this group of the needy is not suitable for children. Recruit seasoned listeners who are familiar with street people. As a precaution, don't leave valuables or personal items like purses around.

How do you find people in need of the Drop Inn Bus?
Simply park in front of shelters and other places where the needy gather, and they'll make their way to you.

74 FOOT CARE

Jesus did it. The apostles did it. The early church apparently did it to one another during their gathering times. Foot washing has been a part of church culture from the beginning of the church itself. But have you considered aiming your foot washing beyond the walls of the church and out to the community?

WHAT YOU'LL NEED

☐ Water
☐ Soap
☐ Anti-bacterial wipes
☐ Scented lotion
☐ Folding chairs
☐ Nail clippers
☐ Bowls for cleaning
☐ Towels for drying
☐ Drinks for those waiting
☐ Connection cards

Set up a little foot-washing station with a sign that reads, "Free Foot Washing—No Donations!" You'll definitely attract attention and a lot of questions. You might need to wash each other's feet to get the ball rolling.

With a little bit of training, caregivers can also learn to look for infections that might need more serious medical attention.

Foot massages are also part of this ministry. Other elements include:

- New socks
- Praying for folks when you're done
- Talking to your "patient" as you do your foot work

How do you find people in need of foot care?
Check parks where people hang out and homeless shelters. You can also distribute flyers in the neighborhood the morning of the event.

75 DOOR-TO-DOOR PRAYER

Approach people in an unassuming, friendly manner. Nothing is more irritating than a pushy spiritual person who comes across as "holier than thou." On the other hand, the sincere

WHAT YOU'LL NEED

☐ Vibrant volunteers
☐ Connection cards

offer to pray for someone—for a complete stranger, no less—is powerful to the point of bringing some people to tears.

How do you find people who are looking for prayer?
Pray and trust God to lead you to the right places.

76 PRAYER AT MENTAL INSTITUTIONS

Talk to the authorities at the institution to explain what you will and won't be doing. Training as a chaplain might be necessary, though some institutions will allow minimally trained laypeople in as long as they're spon-

WHAT YOU'LL NEED

☐ Patient volunteers
☐ Connection cards

sored by a church. This can be as simple as setting up a "Prayer" sign at a facility.

How do you connect with people who are open for prayer at a mental institution?
Go to mental institutions. Explain your project to the chaplain. Make sure you come across with a serving spirit. Permission from the institution is required. They should be able to identify patients who will be receptive.

IN ACTION: Dayton Vineyard Church started twelve years ago, but they were unsuccessful. After eighteen months of trying, they closed down, moved across town, and started over. Pastor Doug Roe felt their primary mistake on their first attempt was that they weren't nearly focused enough on ministry to the needy. So he estimates that they quadrupled their efforts in caring for people in need. It worked! In Pastor Roe's words, "Apparently, everyone wants to hang around with people who want to be friends with the needy."

LEVEL 3
RECONSTRUCTION—CREATING NEW ECONOMIC AND LIFE OPPORTUNITIES

THE PROJECTS AT THIS level are all about helping others to rebuild their lives in practical ways. In fact, this is perhaps the most important of all of the "R" words we've used to describe these levels of service.

When you're dealing with the needy, you're often working with people whose lives have been destroyed at multiple levels. They usually don't need just a minor repair or a bit of renovation here and there. They often need complete reconstruction from the ground up. They need to learn to think differently and to relate differently to others and to society around them. They may need skill development that has, in many cases, been missing from the very beginnings of their lives. Some individuals come from families where not a single positive model has been present in generations. You could easily be starting at less than zero—in deficit range— with these precious souls.

Remember, God loves people. And he just might connect you with someone who needs this level of involvement and use you to bring healing to that person's life.

MAKING CONNECTIONS WITH COMMUNITY SERVICES
No one can do it all.

As you serve people in need, you'll quickly find out that the situations you'll face are complicated. You'll learn that you simply can't meet all these needs. It's far more helpful if you specialize in what you do best—and be knowledgeable in what other volunteer and community resources are available for needs you can't meet.

The Need for Advocacy
People bring complex problems. Trying to organize what to do, who to call, and how to ask can be particularly overwhelming,

especially if the needy individual is in a crisis. Your role can be as an advocate, helping the needy individual cut through red tape and get through the processes required to receive additional help.

The Need for Wrap-Around Services
Because of budget cuts, many organizations have been forced to cut wrap-around services. These services include such things as coordinating and connecting the activities individuals receive from various providers and community agencies. They also include advocacy services, such as helping individuals fill out appropriate paperwork to receive benefits or services, helping them to understand what services are available to them, helping them to find transportation to health-related appointments, and following through with them after referrals. As wrap-around services have been dropped in community mental health agencies, many people in need of these services are "falling between the cracks."

Connections to Current Support Systems
Before offering new resources to people in need, explore their current support system. Nearly everyone on public assistance has a caseworker. This caseworker can provide many services. If someone isn't connecting with his or her caseworker, explore the reasons why. If the needy person is a veteran, the Veterans Administration has many services available he or she can tap into. Is he or she a senior citizen? Most communities have a vast array of senior services. Explore specific support systems.

How to Find Community Resources
United Way. Contact your local United Way to find out what resources and organizations they have contact with. There is usually a minimal charge for the hard-copy manual. There may be a United Way website for your area, which you can find by going to the national website (www.unitedway.org).

Community Directory. Most communities have listings of specific agencies that are available to help in that county. These can often be obtained through local police stations or community health departments. They list phone numbers of local crisis hotlines, legal assistance providers, domestic violence hotlines, and so on.

The Top Ten Services People Request (in Order of Importance)
1. Emergency financial assistance (rent/utilities)
2. Housing (low-income permanent/shelters)

3. Medical (underinsured/uninsured)
4. Job search/career information/continuing education
5. Counseling/substance abuse (with no insurance)
6. Furniture
7. Domestic violence/family crisis
8. Transportation
9. Crisis pregnancy care/day care
10. Legal aid[12]

What many people really want is someone to listen to and care about them. Even though they don't always know it, they are looking for relationship.

Create a Community Resource Book of Your Own:

- Contact the United Way to find a few really good sources for each of the top ten categories above. Research the resources so that you know where individuals can receive the help they need.
- Contact volunteers who are social workers or medical personnel to find out what resources they've found most helpful in your community.
- Network with people providing community services to find out more about what they do, as well as to let them know what services you offer.
- Research the process of how to receive public assistance with food stamps, housing, medical cards, disabilities, and so on, so you can better help people get into the system.

77 CAR BUYER

WHAT YOU'LL NEED

In today's culture, owning a car is often a necessity for people to have adequate economic opportunity in life. If you've bought more than one

☐ A trusting relationship

car, you've probably made a bad deal that caused you to walk away from the deal shaking your head and feeling taken advantage of.

Don't assume that women don't know how to purchase a car. In our family, for example, Janie always does the car buying. I

(Steve) have never bought a car by myself. She is a savvy negotiator. If I were to lose her, I would be vulnerable to getting ripped off.

Unscrupulous car salespeople tend to take advantage of needy people because they know that these individuals are strapped for loan options. An advocate representing the needy person increases the likelihood of a positive outcome.

If you're a savvy business leader who loves to negotiate and who can walk away from a sale if not satisfied, you'll do great at this ministry. You will want to have significant conversations in advance of the trip to the car lot regarding price range, options, and an agreement that you are willing to walk away from the deal no matter how emotional the circumstances become.

How do you find people who need a car purchased for them?
Check with people who attend your church who have recently been widowed or divorced. During this vulnerable period just after the loss of a spouse, cars often break down (perhaps it's spiritual warfare) and the surviving spouse needs to make a major auto purchase. Also check with people who are already being served by your other ministries to the needy.

78 LITERACY FOR NONREADERS OR SLOW READERS

A surprising number of adults in the United States can't read sufficiently to get or maintain a decent job. Their lack of reading and writing skills keep them stuck in an endless series of low-paying jobs.

WHAT YOU'LL NEED

☐ Curriculum
☐ Facility
☐ Connection cards

This ministry can be very fulfilling for a person who is patient, caring, and enthusiastic. You'll find an abundance of materials, and they come in a variety of formats depending on teaching style and the needs of the student. To explore materials available, check out the very thorough website www.literacy.org.

How do you find people in need of literacy help?
Put the word out by flyers and simple word of mouth. You can also provide a great service to employers because you will help them keep employees, so connect with large local employers who use unskilled and low-skilled laborers.

79 LITERACY FOR IMMIGRANTS AND REFUGEES

One of the primary challenges for newcomers to the United States is the language barrier. The English we speak in this country is particularly difficult to learn because of the many idioms we use in everyday speech. Special training is needed because very few people will catch on to our lingo without some significant language help.

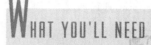

WHAT YOU'LL NEED

☐ Curriculum
☐ Facility
☐ Connection cards

Many of the people coming to this country who need ESL help (English as a Second Language) speak Spanish as their native tongue. The number of Spanish-speaking people will continue to increase dramatically all over the nation. Getting students and building trust in the Hispanic community may be your biggest obstacle.

Two very good resources that offer ESL programs are these websites: www.englishonline.net and www.eslcafe.com. Go to the resources sections of these sites. Choose a couple of resources and begin where you are inclined. With a bit of energy and a little patience, you'll have some success.

Our church has an ESL program that is staffed both by professionally trained Spanish speakers and educators and by people who are simply available and enthusiastic. Both are effective.

How do you find immigrants and refugees in need of literacy help?
Find foreign-language speakers and ask if they would like to learn to speak English *better*. Virtually all are initially interested. Make sure individuals understand that you are church people and are not connected with the government and are therefore "safe."

80 MENTORING CHILDREN

WHAT YOU'LL NEED

Many after-school mentoring programs exist, but have you considered the two-edged sword of training teens to mentor elementary-age students? Both end up coming out on top and are changed by the experience.

☐ Facility space (rent a storefront)
☐ Energetic teenage volunteers
☐ Adult overseers

Teens shouldn't just be token leaders—they can run the entire program, with adults supporting them emotionally, financially, and spiritually.

An after-school program can focus on a particular people group, such as migrant farm workers, inner-city African-Americans, Appalachians, refugees, Hispanics, or agricultural-oriented kids.

How do you find children who need an after-school mentoring program?
Locate in at-risk neighborhoods and ask counselors or principals in local schools.

IN ACTION: Ginghamsburg Church in Tipp City, Ohio, has an extensive ministry to at-risk neighborhoods all over the north Dayton area. This ministry runs most school days and most summer days. What they call "the Clubhouse" focuses on the following elements:

- Character development
- Tutoring—especially study skills
- Six-week classes on cooking, ballet, tennis, swimming, car repairs, computers, music lessons, or cheerleading

To check out what Ginghamsburg Church is doing with the Clubhouse, see their website at www.ginghamsburg.org and look under "Ministries for You: Youth."

81 SERVE (YOUR CITY) WEEKEND

Imagine churches from all over your community working cooperatively to show God's love in practical ways to the entire city. The needy will be touched on a broad scale by the thousands. It's a blitz, going into the community in a number of creative ways to engage

WHAT YOU'LL NEED

☐ Special connection cards

the needy—giving free soft drinks, offering free car washes, painting front doors, and picking up trash. Several dozen churches band together for about two hours with the combined effect of presenting a unified image of the church to the city. Thousands are touched with the love of Christ, the church is brought together, and countless seeds of the gospel are sown.

For this event, put together and print a special connection card with one set of contact information on it. Consider creating a website for the event and print that on the card instead of a specific church or list of churches. The website will direct people to participating churches. Or put a central phone number on the cards where callers will receive the phone numbers of participating churches.

To look at this idea more closely check out this website: www.servecincinnati.com.

How do you find people to serve at a weekend like this?
Start with local clergy organizations and recruit laypeople through local churches.

82 CAR DONATIONS

Willow Creek, a large church on the west side of Chicago that is geared toward seekers, has done a ministry like this for a number of years, and we've done this in Cincinnati as well.

Many people are stuck at poverty income levels due to lack of transportation. But in this ministry, everyone wins. Those who donate cars to a church will get credit for the fair market value as a charitable donation.

All that is needed for the credit is tax form 8283 for noncash charitable contributions. This can be found at www.irs.gov. Donors estimate fair market value for vehicles, and the organization signs that it has received the

WHAT YOU'LL NEED

☐ An area to work on cars
☐ Dedicated volunteer mechanics

cars. Titles should be transferred to the organization upon donation. The organization should carry liability insurance on cars until they're given away.

Some cars will be ready to give away as is. Others will need some repairs to be "street worthy."

If a donated car is not repairable, you might be able to sell it as scrap metal. A scrapped car can bring in three hundred dollars, more or less, depending on body condition, wheels, tires, engine, and market demand. The cash can be used for repairing other donated vehicles. If scrap buyers won't take it, call the Volunteers of America and they'll find a way to repair it and sell it. (See their website, www.carshelpingpeople.org, for the phone number for your area.)

Consider:

- Can the needy person maintain the car once he or she receives it?
- Does the person have a valid driver's license?
- Can the person demonstrate that he or she carries liability insurance?

How do you find people to give cars to?
You won't have a problem answering this question. The better question is, How do you filter out the right people from the wrong people to give vehicles to? Consider setting up a committee that can use criteria that you establish for the type of person you are seeking to help.

How do you find people who want to give away their cars?
Once you have a system for checking out incoming cars, you'll be able to announce to your church that you are giving away good used vehicles to those in need. Make sure you explain that a tax deduction is available for people who donate cars.

83 DRESS FOR SUCCESS

First impressions count a lot when seeking good employment. This course should equip people with a basic understanding of proper business dress and offer recommendations on stores where people can purchase inexpensive basics. Participants should be able to go into a prospective employer with the "look" that is compatible with the work world. Visit www.dressforsuccess.org for ideas.

WHAT YOU'LL NEED

☐ Trained volunteers
☐ Facility

A couple of texts that are the standards for this area are (for men) *John T. Molloy's New Dress for Success* by John T. Molloy (Warner Books, 1988) and (for women) *New Women's Dress for Success* by the same author (Warner Books, 1996).

How do you find people who are open to being in a Dress for Success program?
This is a fit with the other skill classes you might teach, so promote it along with them. This would be a great final class to teach before "students" go out to seek employment.

How do you find people to teach the Dress for Success program?
Approach people from a business or retail background.

84 GOOD HAIRCUTS FOR WORK

WHAT YOU'LL NEED

For these haircuts, recruit the most highly skilled haircutters you can find. Participants could receive haircuts as a reward for completing an interviewing class (project 95) or a Dress for Success class (project 83).

☐ Hair stylists
☐ Hair-styling equipment

How do you find people to cut hair?
Call salons and see if stylists are interested in donating their time for a community service project to benefit the needy. Consider doing a haircutting clinic three or four times per year.

How do you find people who are in need of a haircut?
Contact social services. Again, funnel "graduates" of your skills classes to this project.

85 SPECIAL SKILLS—COOKING

WHAT YOU'LL NEED

Cooking and baking are becoming lost arts today as fast food and convenience foods have invaded the scene. Sometimes feeding a family can take up a big part of an already tight budget in needy households. Put together a curriculum of healthy and inexpensive

☐ Instructors
☐ Space for instruction
☐ Space to practice baking and cooking

meals that can be doubled, frozen, or divided into two meals (for example, a roast on Sunday and barbecue sandwiches on Tuesday). Emphasize nutrition, meal preparation, and how to stretch your food dollars. Consider a local church kitchen or a community room so you can take the class to a neighborhood in need.

How do you find people to take cooking classes?
Put together a flyer and circulate it throughout the neighborhood. Invite people who are already coming to your other ministries to the needy.

86 SPECIAL SKILLS–CARPENTRY

This class covers areas of carpentry that come in handy in everyday life. Topics include how to refinish furniture, how to stencil walls or furniture, how to winterize doors and windows for energy savings, and simple construction techniques.

WHAT YOU'LL NEED

☐ Space for instruction
☐ Space to practice carpentry
☐ Skilled instructors

How do you find people for basic carpentry classes?
Ask those coming into your other ministries to the needy. Don't confine your invitations to men. Many women will want to learn these skills.

87 SPECIAL SKILLS–SEWING

Another skill that can save money and even make money is sewing. When a needy person learns some mending techniques, he or she gives a whole new life to clothing once considered beyond usefulness. A simple straight stitch learned on a sewing machine can turn raw fabric into curtains, pillows, shower curtains, comforter covers, and aprons. A few more skills—such as sewing zippers, arm holes, sleeves, and buttonholes—can open up a whole new world. Teach people to lay out and cut fabric from a pattern.

WHAT YOU'LL NEED

☐ Space for instruction
☐ Space to practice sewing
☐ Skilled instructors

How do you find people who would like to learn sewing skills?
Ask those coming into your other ministries. Don't leave men out of this one; many skilled "seamsters" are male.

88 SPECIAL SKILLS—COMPUTER INTRODUCTION

Having basic computer skills is no longer just an option if someone is to be viable in the workforce. Having a working knowledge of software such as Microsoft Word, Excel, and Outlook is almost mandatory for people who hope to get hired at decent-paying jobs. In a Computer Introduction class, you can get students so familiar with these programs that they'll be able to walk onto a new job site and feel comfortable using them with little or no assistance.

WHAT YOU'LL NEED

☐ Computers
☐ Software
☐ Patient instructors
☐ Instruction space

The best way to acquire a new skill is to learn by doing. The key to doing with computers is having multiple computers available to students. The ideal classroom setting is a room full of computers with one instructor per four or five students. Consider practice projects that will benefit your church, such as Sunday school class agendas, name and address databases, teaching schedules, newsletters, flyers, and so on.

One option is to give students their own computers at the end of the class as a reward for completion. Out of the question? It might just be doable with the Pass It On—Computers program (project 15).

How do you find people who need to learn basic software programs?
Ask those coming into your other ministries to the needy.

89 SPECIAL SKILLS—CUSTOMER SERVICE

Employees in full-service restaurants—waiting, bussing tables, and hosting—can be well paid. And judging by "Now Hiring" signs, people who can fill these positions are always in demand. But these jobs do take some acquired customer service skills, and attaining these skills comes from practice. Use instructors who are veterans in the restaurant industry. They can show and tell how

WHAT YOU'LL NEED

☐ Skilled instructors
☐ Facility
☐ Equipment for serving

it is done. Then role-play where students serve prospective customers. Be sure to practice some customers who aren't easy to care for. Critique students and practice until students are ready to apply for real jobs waiting on customers, bussing tables, or being hosts.

How do you find people who are in need of learning these and all special skills?
Ask those coming into your other ministries to the needy. Post classes on a job board that your church may provide.

90 JOB COOPERATIVE

When working with the needy, it seems like everyone — sooner or later — is looking for a job. Instead of waiting for the perfect jobs to appear, start your own clearinghouse for jobs — your own job service. With a little effort and organization, you can help many people find employment. You'll also help employers locate a steady stream of workers.

WHAT YOU'LL NEED

☐ A way to post new job opportunities
☐ A way to gather information about new job opportunities

How do you find people who are looking for a job?
Word will travel fast when you succeed at helping people find employment. Begin by advertising in local newspapers, but that won't be necessary for long. Other avenues include apartment complexes or community bulletin boards.

How do you find jobs to list?
Connect with employers in your community and share your vision for your new ministry. Be sure to explain how listing jobs with you will benefit the employers.

91 SHOPPERS FOR THE ELDERLY OR SHUT-INS

One of the most frustrating difficulties for needy people who are confined to their homes is the inability to be mobile to purchase groceries and other needed items.

The shopper calls in once or twice a week to check in on his or her "clients." If you have the time and inclination, you can develop a "drop on by" relationship instead.

This ministry might be low on outward thanks, but it will be very high on inward satisfaction. Try to remember that this is one of those ministries to the "least of these" that Jesus was referring to in Matthew 25:40 ("Whatever you did for one of the least of these . . ., you did for me").

You can be more efficient if you shop for a number of people all at once.

"We must not drift away from the humble works, because these are the works nobody will do. It is never too small. We are so small and we look at things in a small way. But God, being Almighty, sees everything great. Therefore, even if you write a letter for a blind man or you just go and listen, or you take the mail for him, or you visit somebody or bring a flower to somebody—small things—or wash clothes for somebody, or clean the house—very humble work—that is where you and I must be. For there are many people who can do big things. But there are very few people who will do the small things."[13]

—MOTHER TERESA

How do you find people who need shopping help?
Contact organizations that provide in-home meals, such as Meals on Wheels. The same people who need meals delivered will need shopping assistance for other meals of the day.

92 INTERPERSONAL SKILLS—PARENTING

Single parents face some of the toughest ongoing challenges of people with needs. They battle parenting issues alone, and it only adds to their stress that they face most of their other problems alone.

You can effectively impart parenting skills through mentoring relationships with veteran parents. Recruit parents who are both available and humble, and connect them with a single parent who desires a mentoring relationship.

WHAT YOU'LL NEED

- ☐ Patient, available volunteer couples
- ☐ Texts and study guides
- ☐ Facility for holding classes
- ☐ Space for childcare

You can also teach many of the same skills in a classroom setting. Find a convenient location for your students, and try to provide fun childcare at the same time to make it easier on the parents.

A text to consider using is *Boundaries with Kids* by Henry Cloud, et al. (Zondervan, 1998). This book addresses how to help parents and children take responsibility for their own behavior, feelings, and attitudes and how to bring control to an out-of-control family life.

How do you find people who need parenting help?
Through your other ministries to the needy and through local social service agencies.

93 INTERPERSONAL SKILLS–BOUNDARIES

Healthy boundaries provide the foundation for good relationships, safety, maturity, and growth. Consider offering a class on boundaries to help people learn how to develop boundaries and make positive choices for their own growth. Address emotional, spiritual, physical, and mental aspects of healthy and unhealthy boundaries.

WHAT YOU'LL NEED

- ☐ Books
- ☐ Skilled facilitators
- ☐ Leader's guide and videos

A great text to use is *Boundaries* by Dr. Henry Cloud and Dr. John Townsend (Zondervan, 1992).

How do you find people who need a boundaries group?
As you connect with parents struggling with their marriage relationship and with their children, or others who feel their lives are out of control, you'll find people to invite to a boundaries group.

94 INTERPERSONAL SKILLS–CODEPENDENCY

For each person addicted to a substance, a handful of others are connected to that person through a web of codependency.

Codependents are people in close relationship with the addict who inadvertently feed that person's addiction by protecting him or her. The difficulty with codependency is that it feels like you're just giving love to the addict, and you don't realize you are enabling him or her to continue with the addiction. A group for people learning to deal with these issues can be a liberating key to help them mature and grow forward.

W HAT YOU'LL NEED

- □ Books
- □ Facilitator
- □ Meeting place

A great text to use for leading these groups is *Codependent No More: How to Stop Controlling Others and Start Caring for Yourself* by Melody Beattie (Hazelden, 1996).

How do you find people who need help with codependency issues?
As you run into people in your various ministries to the needy, you will find those who are dealing with codependency issues. You will also find many people at Alcoholics Anonymous and Al-Anon meetings who are looking for groups like this.

95 INTERPERSONAL SKILLS–INTERVIEWING

You only get one chance to make a good first impression. Those who consistently land jobs have learned the skills necessary to make that first impression, but others—particularly many needy people—haven't yet learned the basics.

Teach classes on how to dress for an interview, how to handle tough interview questions, how to write an excellent résumé, and how to connect with job placement agencies. Use role-playing, and video tape the practice interviews as a learning tool. Consider job skills inventories and personality inventories to help people know themselves better.

W HAT YOU'LL NEED

- □ Facility
- □ Books

If you'd like to use a textbook, consider *The Complete Idiot's Guide to the Perfect Interview* by Marc Dorio (Alpha Books, 2000).

How do you find people who want to learn interviewing skills?
Connect with people looking for employment.

96 INTERPERSONAL SKILLS—LISTENING

The ability to listen is central to all human skills in getting along with one another, yet very few people know how to really listen. Instead, most people are quiet in conversation only because they're formulating what they're going to say next. People rarely quiet themselves long enough to actually deeply listen to what another person has to say. This predicament seems to be amplified among people who are needy.

WHAT YOU'LL NEED

☐ Books
☐ Meeting place
☐ Patient, skilled leaders

The book *Listening for Heaven's Sake* by Ping and Sweeten (Equipping Ministries, 1993) is a good starting point (available on Amazon.com or through www.kindness.com or at 1-888-KINDNESS). This text teaches how to listen for content and feeling and how to reflect it back to the person who is talking. It covers how to communicate warmth, empathy, and respect. It is also helpful in identifying classic non-listening responses such as The Historian, The I Told You So, The Chicken Soup response, and others. Training videos and teachers are also available from Equipping Ministries International in Cincinnati, Ohio.

Those who can learn to listen will accomplish more and will see new doors of opportunity open for them.

How do you find people who are looking to learn listening skills?
Suggest this course to the people who are already taking your other courses on personal and skill development. This is a great addition for those in need who are growing forward.

This class is also excellent training for anyone involved in ministry.

LEVEL 4
RELOCATION—BECOMING WORLD CHANGERS

Our God is an incarnational God. He doesn't send help—he brings help firsthand. He brings that help through us, his people.

When our church was getting started in Cincinnati, we held a brainstorming session on how we could creatively evangelize our city. One of the ground rules for brainstorming is that there's no such thing as a bad idea. But one guy came really close. He suggested that for a mere ten thousand dollars per season we could rent an air banner (the kind that airplanes pull behind their tails with messages) to fly over the Cincinnati Reds baseball stadium. He believed this air banner would effectively evangelize the entire city in the space of one baseball season (the Reds were having a great season!) with a catchy phrase that said it all, like, "Jesus is Lord over Cincinnati!"

I (Steve) asked him to read John 3:16. Then I asked him why he thought God sent his Son and not an air banner to planet Earth. I know he meant well, but his suggestion revealed a problem we face in the church today. We want to touch a lot of people without inconveniencing ourselves. But it just doesn't work that way. What we need are more heart connections that will allow us to weave ourselves with people at the level of the soul, not more clever ideas that are going to briefly touch people's minds.

That's what this final brief section is about—touching people who need our help at the deepest levels possible.

97 SERVING VACATIONS

Why can't missions be a go-and-do affair for the average person?

"Missions" is a church word, not necessarily a biblical one, though the concept is thoroughly scriptural. The word "missions" doesn't communicate to newcomers to the faith all that well. People in church circles speak about "short-term missions" or about going on a trip to serve at a foreign location for a week or two.

WHAT YOU'LL NEED

□ Connection with a group already working in another country

Why not consider the alternative term "serving vacation"? "Vacation?" you ask. How can going to a Third World country be a vacation?

We've taken several of these serving vacations—most of them to the city dumps of Mexico City to serve the poor there—and we believe there is nothing you can do in the course of a year that will be more selfish. Sure, you can do a lot of good as you complete humbling work on these trips among the poor. But you can also stay in nice accommodations at night and eat in the country's nicest restaurants.

On a serving vacation you'll most often connect with people already serving in another country. Typically, they're doing medical, dental, or optical care. Your group comes to give assistance to what they're doing with manpower and finances.

How do you find people who are looking to take a serving vacation?
Ask around your church. Share your vision. Seek to turn some of your missions efforts into local empowerment.

IN ACTION: Southeast Christian, a giant-sized church in Louisville, Kentucky, has a giant heart for missions. Over the past several years, they have developed something similar to the serving vacation concept. They now offer short-term missions trips to more than a dozen locations around the world. Their people are eating up these opportunities! For an affordable price, they can go on excursions that last between an extended weekend and two weeks. They come back from these trips exhilarated, knowing that they've planted seeds of change that will make a difference in the light of eternity.

98 URBAN FREE STORE

People in need commonly have concerns that extend beyond food and clothing. They also need to set up households, which calls for furniture and appliances. You can approach this ministry two ways—either offer these items completely free or offer them at greatly reduced prices (that is, far less than a used furniture store would sell them for).

Once you put the word out that you're receiving goods for needy people, you'll have many donations. You'll need retail or warehouse space to store and show the goods. Check into grants to cover space, rental, and one employee overseer.

WHAT YOU'LL NEED

☐ Facility
☐ Truck to pick up or deliver large items

Set limited open hours according to the number of volunteers you have.

How do you find people who need an urban free store?
Those who are already coming for food are likely to be looking for furniture and appliances as well.

99 LIVING IN COMMUNITY IN A NEEDY AREA

WHAT YOU'LL NEED

☐ A calling from God to simplify
☐ A calling from God to live in this way together
☐ A calling from God to serve the poor in an unusual way

The motto of those called to this ministry might be, "Making a difference together!" Some people who've experienced ministry to the needy and who feel entirely at home among these special people will feel called to make this unusual commitment. They will feel called by the Holy Spirit to move from their predictable lives and to live among the needy.

How do you find people who are open to moving into a community setting in a needy area?
This is something that God has to put together. No one should even consider this concept unless he or she has been absolutely, clearly, and repeatedly called to this ministry by the Holy Spirit.

100 BRINGING CHURCH TO APARTMENT DWELLERS

There is a crying need for significant churches among the needy. Of the thirty million families in America that live in apartments, between 80

WHAT YOU'LL NEED

- ☐ An enthusiastic team
- ☐ Meeting place
- ☐ Sound system

and 95 percent are totally unchurched for various reasons (transportation problems, lack of relational connection, language difficulties, and so on).[14] Instead of simply sending invitations to an existing congregation, why not bring church to apartment dwellers? The plan is simple, low-tech, and low-dollar. Initially, volunteers come from a sponsoring church to lend their energy. Eventually, workers come from within the apartment community itself.

The apartment manager's cooperation is key. Point out the benefits to him or her: lower turnover rates, more pride and care for surroundings, people helping one another, and so on.

The goal is to meet on-site, *not* to eventually build a building or hire a staff that the congregation could never afford.

How do you find people who would come to a church in their apartment building?
Place flyers in low-income or rent-assisted apartment complexes.

101 URBAN WEEKEND

Some people living in the suburbs may want to serve needy people, but they have fears about going to urban areas to do ministry. This

WHAT YOU'LL NEED

- ☐ Facility
- ☐ Leaders

brief intensive project provides a needed jumpstart, but in a safe way.

Start on Friday evening and end on Sunday afternoon. Assemble your team for a three-day weekend that will ease newcomers into doable ministries to the needy. Part of the weekend includes a series of lectures from various leaders on aspects of ministry to the needy. These talks are balanced with simple projects like the ones in the first section of this book. The team stays overnight in the urban area to get a taste of a neighborhood.

How do you find people who would like to have an urban weekend experience?
Advertise in your church and among other area churches.

TOP TEN PROJECTS TO LAUNCH OUT WITH

1. Vegetable and Fruit Giveaway (36)
If you want something quick with high visibility and momentum, this is for you. Your people will get a charge out of the success of this one.

2. Backpacks for the Homeless (5)
You'll become famous among the homeless with this project.

3. Food Pantry (55)
This is a must when starting a ministry to the needy. It's tough to say that you care for the needy and yet don't care enough to provide food for them.

4. Yellow Bag Grocery Collection at Church (7)
What a great way to connect your church quickly with a doable ministry to the needy! They'll immediately begin to feel that they're doing something significant—and they are.

5. Big Parties (51)
Begin to experiment with these high-energy outings and you'll see the energy level go up for ministry to the needy.

6. Bread Giveaway (2)
This low-cost but practical giveaway will be greatly appreciated by the people who receive the bread.

7. Fixing Up Dwellings (48)
Nothing says love like doing a little fixing up on someone's home. And it really doesn't take much expertise.

8. Nail Care (1)
Simply set up in a park. You'll quickly draw a crowd.

9. Backpacks Filled with School Supplies (6)

One of the best ways to show love to a parent is by blessing his or her children.

10. Door-to-Door Prayer (75)

Prayer is the answer to the deepest human felt needs.

ALPHABETICAL LIST OF THE 101 PROJECTS

NOTES

1. Acts 9:36-42.

2. Quoted by Kenneth I. Woodward, "The Changing Face of the Church," *Newsweek*, April 26, 2001, p. 46.

3. George Barna, *Re-Churching the Unchurched* (Ventura, CA: Issachar Resources, a division of Barna Research Group, 2000), p. 25.

4. "Ann Landers," *Sun-Sentinel* (Ft. Lauderdale, FL), April 14, 2001, 2D.

5. Quoted by Michael Collopy, *Works of Love Are Works of Peace* (Ignatius: San Francisco, 1996), p. 46.

6. Quoted by Collopy, p. 35.

7. Louis Uchitelle, "How to Define Poverty? Let Us Count the Ways," New York Times.com, May 26, 2001.

8. Quoted by Uchitelle.

9. Ronald J. Sider, "Revisiting Mt. Carmel Through Charitable Choice," *Christianity Today*, June 11, 2001, p. 85.

10. Quoted by Uchitelle.

11. Andrew Sullivan, "The Way We Live Now—Counter Culture, A Love Story," *New York Times*, April, 16, 2000, sect. 6, p. 28.

12. Based on information from the Mercy Works Co-op, a ministry of Vineyard Community Church in Cincinnati, Ohio, which serves nearly eight hundred families per month.

13. Quoted by Collopy, p. 135.

14. From Richard L. Dunagin, *Beyond These Walls* (Nashville, TN: Abingdon, 1999). To read more about this idea by people who have done it well, read this excellent book. Chapter 5 specifically deals with this unique approach to "doing church" (pp. 63-83).

ABOUT THE AUTHORS

STEVE and JANIE SJOGREN have been involved in church plant-
ing in Oslo, Norway; Baltimore, Maryland; and Cincinnati, Ohio.
Janie is a graduate of Sonoma State University (California). Steve
graduated from Lutheran Bible Institute of California and Bethany
College (Kansas), and is the author of many books, including *101
Ways to Reach Your Community* (NavPress), *Conspiracy of Kindness*,
and *Servant Warfare* (both Vine Books). The Sjogrens live in West
Chester, Ohio, with their three children, Rebekah, Laura, and Jack.